"Once again, Lynelle Mason has penne
in writing style, research, and intrigue. It holds the reader's interest in
a powerful way as she reveals the ups and downs of her early life. After
writing about many others, lastly my own biography as told by Lynelle,
I read with great interest her account of her own life story up to adult-
hood. I could see many similarities to mine, although our backgrounds
were very different in many ways. She pushed through adversities to
reach her goals. She was supported by strong people who loved her
and encouraged her, with her mother being a central figure. Although
she was only a baby when her father died, the influence of that event
shaped much of the family's life, and therefore, Lynelle's writing style
of bringing in history and current events adds interest and brings rich-
ness to her story. I now understand better the woman whom I call
friend. I so admire someone Lynelle's age who continues to be very
engaged in life and takes on projects that require a lot of work. She is
an inspiration and model for all of us. Instead of resting on her laurels
after a life of many achievements, she continues on an active path.
With the ups and downs of life, what stands out prominently is her
strong Christian faith, which is something for each of us to emulate."
—Phyllis E. Miller, Obstetrician-Gynecologist, Chattanooga, Tenn.

"*My Inheritance* is a candid and heartwarming memoir of childhood
amidst family turmoil and upheaval during the Depression and
World War II. Lynelle Mason invites us to walk with her through
the untimely death of her father, the struggles her mother endured
to keep the family together, and her first steps toward a wider
understanding of the world and the importance of her faith. Carefully
sifting through a trove of memory, she has clearly identified what
was worth keeping and what needed to be left behind. The lessons
imposed by hardship and struggle have not been without value,
and she has done us a great service by sharing those lessons."
—Bill Ireland, Pastor/Executive Coach/Church Consultant, Knoxville, Tenn.

"Lynelle Mason gives us a child's eye view of events from 1931 to 1948. As historically important as the Depression and WWII were in our country's past, Lynelle's clear-eyed view of her family's life is the highlight of *My Inheritance*. The poverty and nomadic life she experienced were undergirded by the deep love of her mother, siblings, and a large extended family. Join Lynelle's journey through South Georgia, as she overcomes a fractured early education to become a confident young woman."—Martha Killian, Former Special Education Teacher, Aiken, S.C.

"To know Lynelle Mason now as an amazingly positive and vibrant person, you would never guess what a difficult and often tragic young life she lived. This is a story of courage, grit, perseverance, and love. *My Inheritance* will inspire each of us to be grateful for those in our lives who have loved us along the way and have pointed us to a loving and faithful God."—Brenda Hooper, Former English and Speech Teacher, Signal Mountain, Tenn.

"I have read all of Lynelle's books and enjoyed them immensely. She always seems to keep me interested as a slow reader. In *My Inheritance*, I appreciate how she speaks candidly about her family's struggles and that God was always with her."—Nibby Priest, Insurance Advisor, Henderson, Ky.

"Lynelle Mason brings her early years to life with her inspirational telling of her story with colorful anecdotes. Her resourceful mother worked hard to keep the family together after her husband's untimely death. You will enjoy Lynelle's list of Santa's gifts such as fiddlesticks and jacks and the big handful of hard candy that a nickel would bring at that time. Lynelle includes her faith journey and how she almost became a Methodist. I commend this entertaining book by a remarkable woman."—Carol Prevost, Former English and Speech/Drama Teacher, Chattanooga, Tenn.

# My Inheritance

Family and Faith
During the Great Depression and World War II

Lynelle Sweat Mason

© 2022

Published in the United States by Nurturing Faith, Macon, Ga.

Nurturing Faith is a book imprint of Good Faith Media (goodfaithmedia.org).

Library of Congress Cataloging-in-Publication Data is available.

978-1-63528-188-0

Cover and interior design by Amy C. Cook.

Cover images:
Top Cover Image: Three generations of the Jordan Family, c. 1920.
Bottom Cover Image: (Left to right) Kathryn, Herbert, and Lynelle Sweat.
Pump Organ on Page 20: Wystan, CC BY 2.0, via Wikimedia Commons.
Image located on this website: https://commons.wikimedia.org/wiki/File:Ann_Arbor_
Organ_Co._reed_pump_organ_(c.1890s).jpg. No changes were made to the image.

# PREFACE

If someone told you that you had inherited a million dollars, what would you say? What would you do? My guess is you'd be leaping in the air with wild thoughts running through your mind of living on Easy Street for the rest of your life.

The things I have inherited, both the good and the not-so-good, have little to do with money. Among my inheritances are the genes given to me by my parents and ancestors. The places where I have lived have left their marks on me, some happy and some sad. Likewise, certain people and events, both sought and unsought, throw additional light on who I am. They all are tied together in a bundle I choose to call my inheritance.

I encourage you to look for inheritance traces throughout this narrative, roughly divided into the following time periods, and also to explore your own inheritance.

*1931–1938*
*1938–1940*
*1940–1942*
*1942–1943*
*1943–1945*
*1945–1946*
*1946–1948*

# INTRODUCTION

Not even America's Great Depression of 1929 that turned the economics of the world topsy-turvy could slow the romantic intentions of Cleo Jordan and Ward Sweat. Cleo lived with her mother and often visited in the home of her married brother, Crawley. Both her mother and Crawley lived in the area that today is known as Dixie Union, situated 15 miles north of Waycross, Ga. Ward lived with his family 22 miles from Waycross in Pierce County, in a rural area sandwiched between the towns of Alma and Blackshear.

In a letter that Ward wrote to Cleo from his home, he exclaimed—with a lot of "ohs!" interjected—how he was yearning to see her and how deeply he was disturbed to hear that she thought he didn't care for her. He bemoaned the single life and attested he would enjoy being married. Throughout his letter he asked Cleo, "Don't you?" Much of his letter involved his trying to figure out when Cleo was going to be home.

(In the 1920s a young man called on a young lady at her home. And, if the two of them were lucky, they could go for a short stroll. Kissing and petting were taboo.)

Cleo was enrolled in a school where she majored in elocution, better known today as speech, and she had just finished a starring role in a school play. Her theatrical career, however, ended when her brother Crawley gave his blessing for Ward and Cleo to marry. Cleo was 17, and Ward was 18. The couple spent their one-night honeymoon at the DeSoto Hotel in Savannah.

Cleo's parents, David Abraham Jordan and Leannie Taylor Jordan, had begun their marriage in a one-room log cabin with a dirt floor, on the land north of Waycross where they would later build a spacious dwelling. By the time Cleo was born, David Abraham had acquired massive land holdings.

Ward's family lived in an obscure part of Pierce County called The Forks of the Hurricane. The unusual name for that area came from a violent storm that tore through a large swath of land in Bacon and Pierce counties and stripped the land of thousands of trees. Although the storm was a tornado, the settlers called it a hurricane and named the resulting barren land Big and Little Hurricane Creeks. The "Forks" part had to do with where the creeks divided into two parts.

The Sweats' house would never adorn the pages of *Southern Living* magazine. Through the years it experienced many growing pains. It probably started with a main bedroom, and later a kitchen and dining room and a huge hallway connecting them were added. The house also boasted an indoor bathroom and a six-party telephone hookup. Electricity provided the family with pumped well water.

Upon the death of her father in 1912, 13-year-old Cleo was given two pieces of property: a farm 15 miles north of Waycross and a house at 602 Miller Street in Waycross, the county seat of Ware County, located 57 miles from the Florida line. First settled in 1820, it was the ninth stop from Savannah on the railroad, and soon became known as "Old Nine." Only much later did the name Waycross stick.

By 1930, Waycross had established itself as a railroad hub for the Southeast and boasted a population of 15,510, nine of whom resided at 602 Miller Street: Cleo Archie Jordan Sweat and John Ward Sweat and their five boys and two girls. On Feb. 24, 1931, Baby girl Sweat (the name that appeared on my original birth certificate) joined the company of this family with deep roots in Southeast Georgia.

John Ward Jr. (J.W. or J. Fudge)

Quentin (Skeet)

Darcile

Harold

Chandos (C.D.)

Kathryn (Tunt)

Herbert

Lynelle (Ninkey)

Join me in experiencing a slice of the small town of Waycross I knew as a youngster.

You have a nickel to spend, and it's burning your hand like hot lead. You can't wait to get to S. H. Kress & Co. "five and dime" store. Alas! as you arrive to cross over Hicks Street to get on Plant Avenue, your eyes and ears are bombarded by a train engine going chugga, chugga, chugga, choo choo! The friendly engineer waves and toots his horn: waank, waank, waank! I wave back and begin staring at the too-many-to-count cargo cars snaking behind the engineer's elevated seat.

Suddenly the air space darkens as billows of black smoke descend upon me. I close my eyes, hoping to escape the tiny bits of flying sparks coming from the boiler. Finally, I spy the little red caboose and begin smacking my lips in anticipation of the huge display of mouth-watering candy I will soon gaze upon once the train passes and the tracks are clear. Digging in with my bare feet and running as fast as I can, I waste no time finding the five-and-dime store.

When I get to the candy counter, I point to the peanut butter kisses and show the clerk my nickel. She begins filling a quart sifter with the brown, individually wrapped goodies. When it is crammed full, almost to the point of over-flowing, the purchase is completed. Clutching my bag of candy, I skedaddle home.

The laid-back, safe, family-friendly community of Waycross in the 1930s–1940s is part of my inheritance. So, too, is the small but comfortable wood-frame house on Miller Street with a modest front porch. It had electric lights and a commode, but no bathtub. And a major part of my enduring inheritance is the family that lived in this simple house, a family cemented together with love.

# 1931–1938

## One Bolt of Lightning

On July 19, 1931, a love affair formed by Cleo and Ward for 14 years came to a screeching halt! I was only four months old at the time, but my family told me the story in the years to come.

Mama, who usually went with Daddy when he preached at Pleasant Valley Baptist Church, 27 miles south of Waycross, wasn't feeling well. My 13-year-old brother, John (who was better known as J.W.), volunteered to stay home and take care of Mama. My 12-year-old brother, Quentin (who went by the name of Skeet), leaped to his feet and offered to accompany Daddy to church.

Our 1924 Ford Model T had to be started by hand. Skeet, who adored Daddy, took note of every move Daddy made. When all the inside levers were in place, Daddy inserted the key and went

Daddy

to the front of the car and began with his right hand to crank the engine. They were lucky: After 10 cranking attempts, the Model T began purring!

As the two of them rumbled down the dirt roads southward at a speed of 20 m.p.h., Daddy fell to singing a popular religious song first published in 1928. The lyrics of "I Shall Not Be Moved" were simple and the tune easy to remember. By the time Daddy had sung the second verse, Skeet joined in on the chorus: "just like a tree planted by the waters. I shall not be moved."

Upon arriving at the church, Skeet quickly connected with some of his buddies to arm-wrestle. As soon as the pianist began playing, however, he rushed to the front row, ready to soak up every word Daddy uttered.

When the church service ended, Skeet and Daddy joined deacon Hughey Dixon and his wife Mattie for dinner at their home. Skeet rubbed his tummy when his eyes fell on the table laden with fried chicken, green beans, corn on the cob, fried okra, vine-ripe tomatoes, homemade biscuits, banana pudding, and sweet tea.

After dinner Mattie Dixon gathered her brood of eight children and Skeet and left to visit some neighbors, leaving the two men alone in the house.

Shortly after Mattie and the children left, a violent South Georgia thunderstorm began pelting the homestead with rain. The heavens rumbled with thunder, and bolts of lightning streaked across the sky. Daddy and Hughey moved to the open back door while continuing to share thoughts heavy on their minds.

What happened next left an indelible mark on the life of my family, our kinfolk, a congregation of believers, and neighbors and friends. Daddy had no sooner finished saying "I have a wife and eight children, but I believe that where there is a will, a way will be made" when a bolt of lightning dropped from the sky. In one split second that bolt of lightning snuffed out the life of my daddy.

---

*Harry Dixon, a Georgia state representative from 1962 to 2000, shares this account of that fateful day as told to him by his father, Hughey Dixon: "The last thing I remember was my foot striking an open rafter supporting the tin roof before I lost consciousness. Later, I gradually regained consciousness and saw the scorched hair in the air from the lifeless body of Reverend Sweat, which was on top of me. I maneuvered myself out the door through a puddle of water and crawled to a fence row and was able to attract the attention of a neighbor."*

---

The Dixons took Skeet to their home, where a crowd as far as the eye could see had gathered. Skeet ran to Daddy's lifeless body and begged, "Daddy, say something! Talk to me!"

Putting her arm around Skeet, Mrs. Robinson, a friend of the family, told him: "Ban and I will drive you home. Your mama is going to find your daddy's death hard to believe."

Skeet agreed. The trip back to Waycross seemed to move at a snail's pace. Skeet never ceased crying while Mrs. Robinson continually smothered him with hugs.

When they arrived at our house, Mama took one look at Skeet and exclaimed, "What has happened? Why are you crying, and where is your daddy?"

Skeet took a deep breath and buried himself in Mama's waiting arms. After several attempts, he finally blurted, "Mama, Daddy is dead!"

At first Mama refused to believe him. But when she looked into his wild, tear-stained eyes, his words began to sink in. "Oh, no!" she sobbed, "It can't be! Not Ward!" Soon all the children came running to see why Mama was so upset.

Convulsed in a tsunami of tears, Mama managed to gather her children to her bosom. She sent J.W. to get word to her mama and Crawley.

Skeet began biting hard on his lower lip. "When Mrs. Mattie brought us to her house, I found Daddy lying on the rain-soaked ground not too far from the back porch. Mama, Daddy was not breathing!"

Mama sent Darcile to tell her sisters—Maude, Annie, and Minnie—the awful news. In less than 30 minutes the house was overflowing with mourners. As the news spread of the sudden death of one of the town's most promising young ministers, a group began converging in the area adjoining our house.

Finally, the funeral plans were completed. Daddy lay in state for 24 hours in the parlor of his parents' home in The Forks of the Hurricane. A steady stream of kinfolk and visitors came to pay their respects. Daddy's brothers watched over his corpse during the midnight hours. The following day we held a funeral service in Pierce County at Beulah Baptist Church, Daddy's church when he was growing up, where he became a Christian, and where he had once served as pastor.

More than six ministers spoke long and hard at the service, and their main emphasis was not on consoling the grieving family but rather on exhorting the listeners to be prepared for Judgment Day! Musical selections included "The Old Rugged Cross," "I'll Meet You in the Morning," "Will the Circle Be Unbroken?" "I Shall Not Be Moved," and "Farther Along." The service closed with "Precious Memories" being sung as mourners as they passed by the open casket for a final goodbye.

---

*In the 21st century we tend to major on celebrating the life of the deceased while offering consolation to those most bereaved. While there are seldom wakes in people's homes today, individual churches often employ beautiful, symbolic rituals. In my church, First Baptist of Chattanooga, Tenn., deacons and deaconesses sometimes stand guard by the closed casket for intervals of 15 minutes prior to the burial service. As the casket bearers move the casket from the sanctuary through our vestibule, members of my Sunday School class form a long line as a visible sign we have lost someone dear to us. Regardless of the different approaches to death, in any age, giving up someone dear to us is always be a major grief experience.*

---

My grief—and questioning—began at an early age. A minister and a deacon were struck by lightning. One died and the other lived. This story has become a major part of my inheritance. My daddy's untimely death filled me with lifelong yearnings for a father who, in my mind, had been elevated to sainthood. It has led me to ask God questions that most often have ended in silence.

### A Double Loss

Two weeks after Daddy's funeral, Mama's brother Crawley stopped by Miller Street to check on his baby sister and her children. To his dismay, he found Mama wringing her hands. He asked, "Why are you so upset?"

"It's Ward's brother, Alfred," she answered. "He wants me to send all the children except the baby to the new Baptist Children's Home at Baxley. Crawley, I'd rather die than give up my children!"

Crawley's face turned red. "By gum, Cleo! That makes me angry. Alfred has enough money to buy a new car, but he can't find any money to help Ward's children. Shame on him!" While hugging Mama, he added: "Don't you worry. Your children aren't going to an orphans' home! As long as there is bread on my table, you or your children will never go hungry." He paused before adding, "Cleo, I've exhausted everything I know to do trying to salvage your property on Miller Street. The only thing left is to move you to your farmhouse at Dixie Union."

Crawley was true to his word: we did not have to go to an orphans' home. Even so, more tragedy followed. One year after the untimely death of Daddy, Mama's mother died. Ms. Leannie was known throughout the region for sharing bouquets of flowers from her garden with many people. After Daddy's death, Mama had leaned heavily on her mother for loving support.

Another year passed before our fateful moving day arrived. All three of Mama's sisters huddled near Crawley's Ford Model T to bid her *adieu.*

Dixie Union was only a few miles away, but for Mama it might as well have been a thousand miles from her Miller Street neighborhood where three of her sisters lived. She cried all the way to Dixie Union.

Unfortunately for my family, the escapade about sending my siblings to the orphans' home was never forgotten. It is one of the things I have inherited that I'm not so proud to claim!

### Move #1

You could travel a thousand miles and not find a more revealing South Georgia name than Dixie Union. Today that name conjures up images when white supremacy was in full swing and Blacks were okay so long as they stayed in their place. Both races knew exactly what that meant!

I was 2 years old when my family moved from Miller Street in Waycross to Dixie Union. That rural community became the custodian of my happiest childhood memories. My cache of memories cluster around our home at Route 1, Box 66, Waycross, Georgia;

Dixie Union School; Jordan Methodist Church; the village called Haywood, and in particular Haywood Baptist Church.

These happy memories involve my kinfolk but are heavily slanted toward myself, Mama, my maternal aunts, and John Ward Jr. Now, join me on a trip to Dixie Union and our "home, sweet home."

Dial your time button to 1933, crank up your Model T, and let's get on Highway No. 1. After you've driven for 15 miles, you'll spot a sign on your right saying Dixie Union Road. Just in case you're running low on petrol for your horseless carriage, you might want to drive up a few yards beyond the sign and visit Lott's Service Station. You'll find Lott's Store is stocked with a little bit of everything. It's hard to leave the store emptyhanded!

After exiting Lott's, back up your Model T and turn right onto Dixie Union Road. Stay on that road for about five miles until you come to a farmhouse belonging to the Thorntons. Turn left at the Thorntons' farm and soon you'll cross a small creek. Stay on this road for about two miles. Now you can turn off the ignition switch on your Model T and plan on staying for a while.

Our house belongs to the Early Americana or "Let's Get a Roof Over Our Heads" era. The unpainted six-room house has a porch that extends across the front and ends with an artesian well and washstand. The porch continues down the left side of the house until it attaches itself to the pantry and kitchen.

The outer wall of the living room is made of chinked-together logs. Upon entering the house, its scant furnishings are evident. The living room consists of a fireplace, two worn upright chairs, a small table, and a 30-inch portrait of Daddy and my brother Chandos. Daddy is holding his Bible under his arms.

The door to the left of the living room leads to Mama's bedroom. Her iron bedstead. with its two high-rise feathered mattresses, is covered with a handmade Dutch Girl quilt. A massive, long dresser made of ornate wood and housing a mirror stands against the wall.

Now, re-enter the living room. The door opposite the front door opens to a pantry-size bedroom where my brothers Harold, Chandos, and Herbert sleep. (John Jr. is living with our paternal grandparents and attending Blackshear High School some 20 miles from Dixie Union. Skeet is living with Uncle Crawley about two miles from our farm.)

From the boys' bedroom you enter the dining room, where two wooden benches offset an eight-foot plank table, covered in a red-checkered oilcloth. Against the wall stands a wooden safe with screened doors for housing baked goods.

The dining room opens into the kitchen where pine lighter-knots, dipped in rosin, make the cast iron stove turn crimson. A small room to the left of the kitchen is where Mama stores her Mason jars of fruits and vegetables she has canned during their prime seasons.

Directly in front of the gate leading to our front steps are three large sycamore trees. In winter they produce spiked miniature balls. In spring the balls fall to the ground, making a stinky, colossal mess!

In 1939, after seeing the premier showing of *Gone With the Wind* at Atlanta's Fox Theater, John decides our humble abode will be called The Sycamores.

The outhouse, built to take care of life's necessities, is in an area about 500 yards away from the rear of our house. This crudely constructed contraption is 10 feet wide and has three carved-out holes for tending to your business. Unfortunately, it has no screen wiring at the back side to keep away wandering fowl! Our toilet paper,

Lynelle as a preschooler

if you're lucky, is the unused page of a Sears and Roebuck catalog. The only other alternative is to use a corncob. (It isn't any wonder that I put off going to the outhouse!)

Life during the summer months is marked by sweaty bodies and pesky swarms of gnats. Sandspurs, prickly grass plants with sharp points, are known to attach themselves to anything they can find. They are lethal weapons against barefooted boys and girls.

---

*From today's perspective, you're probably wondering why any-one could look back on such a mundane setting with joy. The answer is simple: I felt loved and valued as a person. Those two ingredients are bound to produce good results.*

---

## Memories of Mama

The person who holds center stage and who turned such a barren landscape into a place of highly treasured memories is my moth-er, with her dancing green eyes and a ready smile. I'm told Mama cried all the way from Waycross to Dixie Union. She must have been a master at squashing her personal feelings, because I can't ever remember seeing her cry! Here are a few of my cameo memories of her:

Sewing machine similar to Mama's

- Observing Mama threading her Singer treadle sewing machine and then peddling away until she turned a printed flour sack into a dress for me
- Mama allowing me to keep a kitten, my first pet, that we found near a hill of sweet potatoes
- Watching Mama wring the neck of a chicken (She held the chicken by its feet, took a firm hold on its neck, and then pulled down on the neck and quickly twisted it upward and forward. The chicken's lifeless neck fell to the ground, but the body kept flapping all over the yard. When the flapping ceased, Mama dipped the chicken's body in boiling water and began plucking its feathers.)
- Coming home from school and seeing Mama bent over a large, cast-iron kettle, stirring in lye soap to wash several pairs of overalls
- Whiffing the aroma of freshly baked gingerbread or doughnuts. (Being the baby of the family, I was certain to claim the inner circles of the doughnuts as my own)

- Curling up in Mama's warm, inviting, loving lap and her singing and rocking until I was sound asleep

Such memories aren't erased even during times of family discord. Instead, they create a longing that becomes a relentless search for yesterdays.

### Shirley Temple Curls

I get all goose-bumpy when I begin peeling back the pages of my life to discover my first conscious memory. This event unfolds in Waycross at a beauty shop where young females were practicing, hoping to become beauticians. I have no idea how I got to Waycross from Dixie Union. Perhaps my first cousin Charles gave Mama and me a ride. I do know that Charles, Uncle Crawley's son and my brother Skeet's buddy, was very fond of Mama and delighted in giving her rides back and forth from the farm to Waycross.

Shirley Temple

I vividly remember sitting under a gigantic machine dedicated to giving a straight-hair lassie like me Shirley Temple curls. Why, you ask, did someone want me to have Shirley Temple curls?

Shirley Temple was a dimpled, curly-haired girl who could sing, dance, and act. From 1934 to 1938, wearing her hair in ringlets, she was a beloved Hollywood child actress. I suppose many American mothers dreamed of their daughter becoming a Shirley Temple look-alike.

The sight of that monster-like machine sent goosebumps up and down my spine. The heated curlers dangled down several feet from a circled center. Because I was so young, the assistants hoisted me on top of a pile of towels after shampooing my thin mop of hair. It seemed like I waited an eternity while the staff, made up of students learning the trade, occasionally checked on me. Meanwhile, several of my curlers became unhinged and I made an attempt to alert someone that a blister was forming under one of the curlers.

(Left) 1930s permanent wave machine (Center) Lynelle gets a perm (Right) Three of the young Jordan sisters: Minnie, Cleo, Estelle

I don't remember getting any Shirley Temple curls—maybe a tiny frizzle—but I do recall my Aunt Annie, who ranked first in my list of favorite aunts, waiting for me with a hand-me-down doll carriage and a ragdoll her daughters had outgrown.

Each of Mama's sisters—Annie Lou, Belle, Maude Cinderella (referring to an inherited family surname and not a fairy tale character), Minnie, and Flora Estelle—were strong building blocks of love and affirmation throughout my childhood and youth. Annie Lou was grown and married when Mama was born. She was tall and had an impish grin. When she smiled, little crinkles popped up around her eyes.

## My Brother John

In 1935, at age 4, my interest in goblins and ghosts had grown by 20 notches. "Mama," I asked, "Do ghosts and goblins really run wild on Halloween?"

Mama gave me her most serious look and responded, "I hear tell that devils dressed in red suits and armed with pitchforks have been seen by mean little children on Halloween."

I was about to believe her until she began laughing. "Aw, Mama, you're teasing. There aren't any ghosts, goblins, or devils in red suits... Are there?"

Before Mama could answer, there was a thunderous banging coming from the window in our living room. It sounded like rain pelting down on a tin roof.

"Mama," I asked, "what's that noise?"

Mama pretended she hadn't heard a thing. She rolled her big green eyes and asked, "What noise?"

"That noise. It sounds like it's coming from the window."

"Hmm," said Mama. "I don't know. Let's go see."

I grabbed hold of Mama's apron as she ambled over to the window.

"Oh, my!" I screamed. "That scarecrow is very, very ugly. Mama, don't let him get me. Make him go away!"

"That wouldn't be nice, would it? He can't help being ugly. Maybe he's friendly. Let's go outside and see what he wants."

"I'm not going out there to meet him."

As Mama walked toward our almost-wraparound porch, I began having second thoughts. "Mama," I yelled, "Wait for me. I'm coming."

That horribly ugly scarecrow gave my siblings and me a merry chase. Once he almost had me in his flaying arms. Finally, he left.

Soon, my brother John arrived. He seemed to know nothing about our scarecrow visitor. To heighten our excitement, he draped a quilt over the front porch swing and told ghost stories to Kathryn, Herbert, and me. We all held our breath as John waxed eloquent about someone whose toe had been chopped off and was looking for his missing toe. In mournful tones the giant kept saying, "I want my toe ..." The punchline found the giant saying, "I'll scratch out your graveyard!" and with John reaching out to suddenly grab all three of us. We responded by screaming as if we owned the missing toe. I don't know about Kathryn and Herbert, but right then and there I peed in my pants.

Mama then appeared with a fresh batch of chocolate fudge, and we all gathered in the living room to enjoy it.

I was fortunate that in my early days I had not one but two heroes. I felt as if I was 10 feet tall when John would hoist me on his shoulders and we'd travel around the house with him singing one of his favorite ditties about a sassy little girl who "went right up to the preacher's face, chewing her chewing gum." Perhaps it was because he was the oldest and I was the youngest that there was always a special chemistry between the two of us. He nicknamed me Ninkey, a name that stuck. He had a special knack for making not just me, but all of us feel special.

### Yes, Kathryn, There Is a Santa Claus

Mama tucked Kathryn and me in bed saying, "Go to sleep quickly. Santa won't come while you're awake."

As soon as Mama shut the door, Kathryn (who was 8 years old) began nudging me (who was almost 5), saying. "I want to tell you a secret." My eyes popped open, and I sat upright in our bed. Kathryn continued, "There isn't a Santa Claus! I overheard Mama talking with Harold and Chandos. She told them, 'Find a flashlight and come with me to the barn.' When Mama leaves, I'm going to get up and follow them."

Kathryn couldn't have shocked me more if she'd told me dogs could fly. "Shame on you," I scolded. "You're wrong. When I went with Mama to Waycross, I saw Santa. He was wearing a red suit trimmed in white fur. He even gave me a candy cane."

Every time I came close to falling asleep, Kathryn would poke me in my ribs. She was determined to stay awake and was insisting I join her.

I scooted to the foot of the bed, curled myself up into a knot, and soon was fast asleep. Likewise, Kathryn, despite her best intentions, finally fell asleep.

Dawn had not fully shown its face when I awoke and dashed to the living room. Lo and behold! Santa had paid us a visit. I stuffed a big jawbreaker in my mouth and raced to rouse my sleeping brothers. I had no sooner opened the door to their bedroom than I tripped over the slop jar (pee pot). Plop! My jaw breaker fell into the pot. Not to be deterred, I regained my composure and continued sounding the alarm. It wasn't long before I had everybody up.

Santa brought me paper dolls, jackstones, fiddlesticks, a chalkboard, and a rubber doll.

Although the nearest sidewalk was more than 15 miles away, Santa brought my oldest sister Darcile a pair of roller skates.

Darcile, who was a little on the hefty side, put on her new skates. When she reached the front porch, she lost control and wound up in the yard with her skates bent beyond repair.

Yes, Kathryn, there is a Santa Claus! The magic of Christmas exists whenever and wherever love goes on a lavish rampage and insists on making a difference.

### Aunt Maude Cinderella Jordan Newman

I remember with delight my visits to my Aunt Maude Newman's house on in Waycross. It was the first house to the right of the huge arch that spanned Reynolds Street. The arch of white stucco had blazoned on it in mammoth black letters "Dixie Highway."

I fell in love with my aunt's tiny handmade red chair that had belonged to her now grownup teenagers. I loved sitting in that chair while watching her daughters preen before the dresser mirror. To quote Goldilocks, "This chair is just right." I also enjoyed sitting in the front porch swing. When my sister Kathryn also visited, we would sit in the swing and play a game in which the first one of us to spot a red car got to pinch the loser.

Once when I was visiting Aunt Maude, I came down with what was known as the croup. Since a doctor lived across the street, she arranged to take me to the office at his house. The doctor laid a wooden spoon under my red-flamed tongue and then gave me a tablespoon of a cure-all purplish syrup. (It must have worked. My second bout of sickness did not happen until years later.)

During one of my solo visits to Aunt Maude's I remember my Aunt Annie also being there. I don't recall my exact age at the time. Let's just say this memory ends in my making a conscious moral judgment and never once feeling remorse!

Waycross had a famous barbecue cafe owned and operated by a Black family. Each barbecue sandwich sold for five cents. When it came time to take me home to The Sycamores, we stopped at Jim's Barbecue to place our order. I enjoyed watching my giggling aunts pretending to hide and hoping none of their white friends saw them devouring their mouthwatering delicacies. Aunt Annie also purchased a glass container of assorted candy sticks and told me, "This is for your brothers and sister who didn't get to come today. You can have one stick of candy, but be sure you give the rest to your sister and brothers."

When we arrived at The Sycamores, neither of my aunts had time to stay for a visit. That left me and the jar of colorful candy! I wasted no time popping one of the canes in my mouth, and also found it easy to vary my aunt's instructions. I gave each of my brothers and my sister one candy cane, and boldly claimed the rest as mine. You might say I was willing to sell my soul for a candy cane. (Before you judge me too harshly, you need to know that candy canes were rare in my household.)

## A Store on Wheels

When a rolling store parked near our thatch of sycamore trees, I could hardly contain myself. "Mama, Mama," I cried, "A house on wheels is in our front yard."

Mama stopped what she was doing and went to see what had me so excited. "That house is a store where we can buy or trade for things we need. Let's pay them a visit. You'll be surprised at all the goodies they have."

Our store on wheels was shaped like a box. It had no windows, but it did have a door that served as an entrance and exit.

Mama cautioned me, "Look to your heart's content, but don't touch the merchandise with your hands."

The store had small bins of flour, meal, and sugar. One section had eggs, pecans, and a hodge-podge of fruits and vegetables. A tiny corner had all sorts of sweet treats, chewing gum, and containers of Prince Albert tobacco and snuff. The store even had underwear, overalls, shirts, and a cage of cackling chickens.

Mama swapped a chicken for some kerosene and flour, and I came away the proud possessor of a king-size lollipop.

## Aunt Mary Belle Jordan Rowland

Aunt Belle's house reminded me of our house at The Sycamores. Her house was unpainted and scantily furnished. It stood on the main thoroughfare from Waycross as you approached the community of Dixie Union. Not far from her farm stood the white-frame school for children in grades 1–8, on land she had donated.

Aunt Belle was 14 years older than Mama. She wore her hair plaited in an arc that encircled her face. If you made judgments merely on physical characteristics, you would never have thought she and Mama were sisters. They were also different in other ways.

Aunt Belle moved at an ant's pace and seldom laughed. Mama, on the other hand, moved quickly and enjoyed telling stories. Mama, like my eldest brother John, was always turning lemons into lemonade.

Aunt Belle had three children—one daughter and two sons. One of her prized possessions was an upright piano, and her youngest son, Jack, delighted in sharing with us his rendition of "Chopsticks."

Aunt Belle was the organist for Jordan Methodist Church in Haywood, named in honor of her parents/my grandparents, David Abraham and Leeanna Jordan. For most of his life my grandaddy was associated with Primitive Baptists, or what Mama called Hard Shell Baptists. (She said he was waiting to have a dream to confirm his conversion.) I remember going only once to a dinner on the ground near one of their churches. I peeked inside long enough to watch them washing each other's feet. (In his later years, under the encouragement of my grandmother, my granddaddy became a Methodist.)

### School Days Begin

Lynelle in 1st grade

Brushing aside my dangling bangs, Mama said "I find it hard to believe my baby is old enough to go to school." Turning to Kathryn, she added, "Let your sister sit by you on the bus. And when you get to school, take her to her room."

Kathryn, a full-fledged 3rd grader and known to our family as Tunt, nodded her head to let Mama know she understood.

Herb, looking very worried, pulled on Mama's arm and said with dismay: "This could only happen to me! They're adding a primer grade this year for the first time at Dixie Union. Ninkey and I will be in the same room. Make sure she understands that when it's time for recess, I don't want to play marbles with her. The boys will call me a sissy if I play with her."

Their conversation ended abruptly when the bright yellow, Bluebird school bus arrived at The Sycamores. The driver blew the horn on the bus repeatedly: Beep, beep, beep! The horn seemed to say, Hurry up! We haven't a second to waste.

Armed with my new Blue Horse writing tablet and a number 2 pencil, I raced toward the bus.

Kathryn grabbed my free hand and led me down the aisle to where there were two side-by-side seats.

Herb, a temper-tantrum waiting to explode, strolled to the back row of the bus where the guys congregated.

The bus driver revved the engine and we picked up speed, rumbling down the unpaved road for about a mile before turning onto a seldom traveled side road surrounded by a cluster of pine trees. A little girl with natural curls and soft brown eyes was waiting by her mailbox.

Kathryn whispered in my ear, "That's Eva Mae Tanner. Her daddy is a moonshiner."

"Moonshiner?" I asked. "I don't understand."

Tunt lowered her voice. "He makes whiskey, a bad drink, according to Mama. I hear he's known to shoot his gun in the air when people he doesn't know come prowling around his place."

It wasn't long before the bus was full of giggling girls and boys wearing scowls and wishing they could be anywhere else in the world but on their way to school. We had one more stop to make. Lined up and frowning were three people. All three of them looked as if they had just gotten out of bed and hadn't combed their hair or washed their faces. Their ragged clothes seemed too little for their chubby bodies. The youngest child, named Lucille, appeared to be my age.

Pointing to her, I asked, "What's wrong with her eyes?"

"Mama says she's cross-eyed. She was born that way, and she can't help it."

"Is that big girl and boy with her going to school?"

"Yes," replied Tunt. "And don't act surprised when you see Grace sitting with the 1st graders. She can't seem to pass the

1st grade. Be sure you don't make fun of her. They say she has a bad temper and lashes out when people make fun of her."

In less than 10 minutes the driver parked her bus. As soon as she released the lever to the door of the bus there was a mad scramble to get off. Tunt held me back, and we took our time departing.

Dixie Union School was a white-frame building with a left and a right wing connected in the middle by a large auditorium and a few offices. The left wing housed grades 1–4, and the right wing housed grades 5–8.

(Top) Dixie Union School (Below) A desk similar to Lynelle's in 1st grade

Minutes later someone Tunt identified as an 8th grader began pulling on the rope attached to the large cast-iron bell. "Ding, dong, ding, dong" echoed the big bell hoisted high on a sturdy pole, sending everyone scurrying to find their classrooms.

I kept my eyes peeled on Tunt. She brushed up against me and said, "Don't worry. Before I do anything else, I'll take you to your classroom and introduce you to Miss Lee."

As we moved closer to my room, I tried to hide my feelings. Finally, I asked, "Tunt, what if my teacher doesn't like me, and what if the other kids don't like me? What will I do?"

"You don't have anything to worry about. Your teacher is going to like you, and so will your classmates."

Tunt introduced me to Ms. Lee, and I took a seat in my nailed-to-the-floor desk in front of Eva Mae Tanner. In no time the two us were talking about everything important, such as paper dolls, jump roping, and jackstones. Meanwhile, Tunt eased away to find her class; Eva Mae and I never knew she had left.

Ms. Lee had a prominent nose and a chiseled chin. She seemed to always be adjusting her glasses. She came over to us girls and said, "I'm glad to see the two of you like each other."

Ms. Lee taught us to read using the sight method. I seemed to catch on to her way of teaching reading so much, that at the end of the school year she decided to let me skip 1st grade and be promoted to 2nd grade.

She also had us to participate in plays. I remember being envious of the beautiful, sparkling fairy wings of my blond-haired friend, Bertha Jordan. I couldn't get my wings to stay attached to my shoulders! I think that was the same year that Tunt, who as Red Riding Hood's big bad wolf, had only one line in a play—and that was to howl. When it came Tunt's time to howl, her voice froze and she couldn't even produce a whimper!

Ms. Lee had specific rules when it came to going to the outdoor privy stalls that lay some 500 feet away from the back of our left wing. The privy had five individual stalls. We all knew the rules: Raise one finger if you have to pee, and two fingers for a bowel movement.

For more than 30 minutes I sat at my desk twisting and turning, trying to put off raising my finger so I could be excused. Suddenly, the dam broke. My body urges took over, and I began peeing rapidly. Before I stopped peeing, a tiny lake of smelly urine had formed around my desk!

(Left to right) Kathryn, Herbert, Lynelle

Eva Mae grabbed a rag and tried to help me dry up my "lake." Meanwhile, my brother Herbert couldn't wait to get home.

As soon as the bus stopped at The Sycamores, he leaped off the bus yelling, "Mama! Mama! Ninkey-Stinky peed in her pants today at school."

Mama and Lynelle with Herbert (left) and Chandos (right)

## Second Grade

Once again, I found myself willing to toss aside all my morals for a bag of candy! I may have had difficulty memorizing my basic number combinations, but I knew full well the value of a penny.

Recess was nearly over when I asked my teacher, Miss Kitsy, if I had time to buy some candy at a small convenience store located off the far end of our expansive school grounds. She said, "You've waited too long. The recess bell is about to ring."

Unhappy with her response, I took matters into my own hands. Grabbing Lucille King by the hand, we raced toward the convenience store. Catching my winded breath, I handed my pennies through the wired fence to the owner of the store and she brought me a handful of Hershey kisses wrapped in silver tinfoil. Then we tore off running, hoping our class was still outside. Alas! They weren't. The school grounds were bare. When we crept inside, everybody was in their seats except the two of us.

Miss Kitsy, tall and attractive, bit her lower lip and motioned for Lucille and me to meet her at the cloak room near the back of the room. Her favorite method for dishing out punishment was a yard stick. When it came my time to receive my punishment, I screamed and yelled like a pig being gutted before slaughter. You can believe Herbert was eager to share that bit of news with the family!

*I must have learned that rules are important, especially to teachers and mamas. In my entire 11 years of going to public schools, I never again got a paddling—at least not at school.*

## Jordan Methodist Church

Two churches played a prominent role in my childhood days: Haywood Baptist and Jordan Methodist. Fortunately for me, they held their services bimonthly and at different times.

Jordan Church is part of my inheritance, bequeathed to me from my mother's kin. The wood-frame white edifice consisted of one center section, with two smaller pew sections jutting off from the main stem. The pulpit area was front central. Kerosene lamps adorned the sanctuary walls, but I don't recall being in a service when they were lit. Outside the church building was a well that furnished refreshing water and time to socialize with our neighbors. A slight distance away was the graveyard where the tallest obelisk in the graveyard belonged to my grandparents.

A pump organ similar to the one Aunt Belle played

At the appointed time on Sunday morning, Aunt Belle—wearing a long, flowing, black taffeta dress that reached to her ankles—would take her place at the organ. Pushing her feet against the pedals, she pumped and shifted her feet. It was time to sing.

Preaching wasn't my favorite part of the service. The preacher's voice rose 10 decibels when he needed to stress a point. He'd walk to and fro across the pulpit area and when he got to the place where he was describing hell, he sent cold shivers up and down my spine.

Mama's favorite way of making me behave during church was to pinch me. She may not have been good at making fairy wings, but she was an expert when it came to pinching!

## Dinner on the Grounds

You haven't lived until you've participated in a "dinner on the grounds" event. The women of Jordan Methodist Church planned for weeks, getting all their ingredients lined up for the very special day.

My mouth starts to salivate as I remember digging into a slice of Mama's many-layered burnt caramel cake! Iced lemonade and tea were served from wooden barrels. It goes without saying there was always an abundance of southern fried chicken. My favorite part of the chicken was the drumstick. There was always an ample supply of macaroni and cheese and gobs of potato salad.

We gathered in little pods with friends we didn't get to see very often. The ladies exchanged cooking recipes, and the men talked about the weather and their crops. We children hurried up the eating so we could play games such as Red Rover, Red Rover and Hide-and-Seek.

In a couple of hours, we re-entered the church and sang and sang.

## Dealing with Rejection

Early on I had definite ideas about sweethearts. One Sunday when we were waiting for the church services to begin, a lad from a prominent family in the community had his mother slip me a slice of her homemade cake. I wasted no time hurling his gift cake onto the floor at the entrance to the sanctuary. It caused a big scene, with me shedding crocodile tears as Mama gave me a sound licking. How could I explain to Mama that it was his older brother, one year my senior, who was my imaginary sweetie?

*What a shame I hadn't heard of Dale Carnegie's book,* How to Win Friends and Influence People, *published in 1936. It seems I knew only one way to express my dislikes—and that was to throw a hissy fit. Shame on me!*

## Move #2

Haywood, like its neighbor Dixie Union, was a small community in Ware County. Mama's Aunt Etta owned most of the property in Haywood. Her family had amassed a goodly amount of wealth by extracting sap from the long leaf pine trees that grew in abundance on their property.

To obtain the sap, a worker would first use a bladed instrument called a hack to cut through the bark about 10 inches below the base and form a cavity to hold the collected sap. With the collecting pan secure, the worker then made two inverted v-streaks above the receptacle. The valuable sap, with its many uses, would be collected on a weekly basis.

We were still living at The Sycamores when Mama learned about seamstress jobs opening in Waycross. For transportation to the job, she would need to board the train at Haywood and for 10 cents ride to Waycross.

Mama wasted no time getting some-one to share-crop our property at The Sycamores and obtaining permission from Aunt Etta for us to temporarily move into one of her vacant houses.

Our new abode in Haywood consisted of six rooms that were well roofed but had no ceilings. We had a living room, kitchen, dining room, three bedrooms, and an outdoor privy.

Mama, 1937

We hadn't been living in Haywood very long when Herbert, Kathryn, Mama, and I decided to explore the large rambling barn adjacent to our house. If we had lingered one minute longer, we would have been crushed. In one split second the old barn heaved its last breath and collapsed!

One time I contracted a nasty cold. Mama had a sure cure for colds. Its name was castor oil, a terrible-tasting, inexpensive laxative used by many people in my early years as a cure for the common cold and just about any other ailment you might imagine.

When Mama left the room to retrieve the castor oil, I scooted out of bed, ran outside in my flimsy nightgown, and crouched under the middle of the house. Herbert, my law enforcement brother, quickly volunteered to bring me to justice. I took the castor oil and got better.

## Questionable Behavior

It was nearing Christmas, and visions of Santa captivated my thoughts. Mama had brought home a newspaper circular full of tempting toy options. Grabbing a pencil and a scarce-to-come-by sheet of paper, I began making Santa a list. Mama warned that Santa could leave me only two gifts. I wrote, erased, and rewrote and rewrote until I wore a hole in my want list. Exasperated, I hopped into bed, wrapping my cold feet around Mama's body. "Mama," I begged, "tell me a Christmas story."

Mama obliged and began reciting Clement Moore's famous poem, "Twas the Night Before Christmas." When she got to the part, "he had a broad face and a little round belly, that shook when he laughed like a bowl full of jelly," I begged, "Mama, do that part again." For some reason I found that part especially funny. I guess it was because Mama had a fat belly and when she got to that part, I could feel her tummy shaking.

I was 6 years old and having a dreadful time waiting for Santa Claus. As a matter of fact, I didn't wait!

Two packages arrived by mail early in December. They were clearly labeled: "Do not open until December 25." One package had Kathryn's name on it, and the other one bore my name.

Christmas was more than two weeks away. I begged and begged until Mama finally relented and let us open our gifts. Both of us had received replica dolls of Princess Elizabeth. Then we rewrapped our gifts.

On Christmas Eve my brother John, who had been working for one year as a clerk typist at the Southern Railway office in Atlanta, arrived by train, and my oldest sister Darcile, who was employed in a five-and-dime store in Waycross, also came to Haywood. Kathryn and I unwrapped our gifts for a second time, as if we'd never seen them before.

John brought a passel of fireworks for the boys. We were in the living room and my brothers were exploring their cache of fireworks. Naturally, I couldn't wait for an outdoor showing, so I struck a match and lit one of the Roman candles. Capable of traveling more than 500 feet in the air, when the rocket began sizzling and popping, John lurched to douse out the flame. As he did, gobs of the rocket's powdery contents landed on his one and only suit.

Lynelle, age 7

My church behavior was even more deplorable! I was 6 when Mama's tenure as a teacher of the card class, a precursor to Sunday School for young children, ended abruptly. It all started when she tried to get me to part with my penny for the class collection. I pitched a "woozie bucket" fit—complete with loud screams, defiant stares, and perhaps a little arm-wrestling. (The woozzie bucket was one of my family's made-up words.) I didn't contribute my penny and Mama, so embarrassed over my tirade, resigned and never again volunteered to teach.

## People of Color

In all my years living in Dixie Union and Haywood, my encounter with people of color was practically nonexistent. I can recall only three incidents, and they were about three men whose skin wasn't pastel white.

One day a Black man came to our house at The Sycamores and knocked on the back door. "Please Misses," he begged, "Can you spare me a little food?"

Mama gave him a plateful of biscuits and bacon. He tipped his old felt hat, saying, "Thank you kindly," and then left.

I was curious as to why he came to the back door instead of our front door. Mama said, "He was showing me his respect and letting me know he understood that white people are better than Black people."

The next encounter I had with a Black person happened when I was 6 years old and living in Haywood.

A man we called "Uncle Freeman" lived in a cabin on the property that was within walking distance of the house Aunt Etta was letting us use. Uncle Freeman was living alone when he died. His only daughter was living in Chicago. Mama whipped up a burnt caramel cake, and I went with her to give the cake to the daughter. She and her daughter, who was about my age, met us at the door. Mama went inside to view the body and to spend some time with Uncle Freeman's daughter. Meanwhile, the little Black girl engaged me in a game of jackstones. When it came time for us to leave, I didn't want to go. I liked my new friend.

On the way home Mama said, "Uncle Freeman's daughter has got uppity since moving to Chicago. I could tell she no longer believes in staying in her place."

The last incident happened in Dixie Union when I was in the 5th grade.

The state of Georgia paid to upgrade its rural roads by using people who were serving time on the chain gang. The prisoners had supposedly committed heinous crimes.

One day I spied a huge Black man, who must have weighed 400 pounds, sitting in the doorway of the barn in front of our house. His black-and-white striped uniform was filthy from all his grubby work on our dusty roads. Attached to his ankle was a huge iron ball.

I panicked. I felt sure he had killed someone, perhaps several people, and if by chance that big iron ball came loose from his ankle he'd head straight for our house! This man was black and a criminal, and I was horrified.

---

*Where had I, at such a young age, learned all this mass of empty, unfounded information. I can excuse myself only a little since systemic racism was a given in my part of America. This is another part of my inheritance I'm not proud to own.*

---

# 1938–1940

August in South Georgia is best described as a little less hot than Hades. In August you discover that your get-up-and-go has got-up-and-gone! Armed only with a funeral-home, cardboard hand-fan, you loll away the day fighting an invading army of mosquitoes and gnats. As you swat away at the invaders, you wipe the beads of sweat dripping over your body parts. And when I was growing up in South Georgia, some folks in the city could cool their bodies with an electric fan and quench their thirst with an icy treat, but those living in rural areas had no such luxuries.

In August of 1938, my family left the rural community of Haywood to move back to Waycross so Mama could earn a living as a seamstress with the Works Progress Administration (WPA), a program begun by Franklin Delano Roosevelt in 1935. He had been elected president in 1932 in a landslide victory over Republican President Herbert Hoover, who most Americans felt had not done enough to help solve the enormous financial problems that had stymied the U.S. after the collapse of the stock market.

President Roosevelt led the U.S. Congress to create numerous programs to provide prompt relief to the unemployed and farmers, while at the same time he invoked economic recovery and regulatory actions. The WPA was the umbrella for many programs our federal government initiated to put millions of Americans back to work. The projects included the building of highways, schools, hospitals, airports, playgrounds, and even sewing centers operated by women. At a time when more than 10,000,000 men were without work, it is estimated that the WPA employed at least 3,000,000 people.

## Move #3

Moving back to Waycross was like going home, although Dixie Union would always be home for me. In addition to the benefits of the Works Progress Administration, our move represented progress of another kind: Bye-bye, outhouse! Hello, indoor plumbing!

For me the most fascinating feature of our new living quarters on Alice Street was the bathroom with its two fixtures my Aunt Maude called a commode and a bathtub. The thing she called a commode was partially filled with water and had something like an oval picture frame, minus the picture, attached to it. She explained, "When you have to tinkle or stinky, you sit down on the open frame. And when you finish your business, you pull the lever on the side— and, swish: what you have done is seen no more!"

We didn't have a stopper for the tub, so I just wadded up some old rags and crammed them in the open drainage spot—and voila! I filled the tub with water and in no time began sliding down the back of the tub and landing with a splash into the refreshing water. My brothers had to manhandle me to get me out of the tub when it came time to eat supper.

For about a month we had the luxury of having a Black maid in charge of cooking. I'm sure her services were a gift from my Uncle Crawley. I remember her warm, mouthwatering vegetable soup and her yummy apple turnovers.

We were in our new residence for only a few days when Uncle Crawley's son-in-law arrived. Clinton was behind schedule in getting his tobacco ready to be cured. He told us, "If you'll help me string my tobacco crop, I'll pay you for your work."

Harold, Chandos, Herbert, Kathryn, and I hopped on the flatbed of Clinton's pickup truck. Barefooted and scantily clothed, we headed for Dixie Union. My job, although necessary, was limited to handing three tobacco leaves to one of the stringers, who in turn attached the leaves with twine to a square wooden pole about two inches thick and 36 inches long. Then the strung tobacco was placed in a barn to air-dry.

It was late afternoon when we returned home. I distinctly remember Clinton paying everybody except me. He must have considered his pay promise a stringer-only commitment!

(Left to right) Lynelle, Herbert, Kathryne, C.D., Harold, Darcile, Mama in 1938

Later, Darcile and I were sitting together in the front porch swing when Harold and Chandos began hurling objects at each other. One of them threw something that landed on Darcile's forehead. Blood gushed forth. I screamed, "You bad boys. Come see what you have done!"

The boys ceased fighting and begged to be forgiven.

My sister's reaction, I thought, was strange. I expected her to be angry. Instead, she seemed sad. After cleaning her wound, she had us to sit in a semicircle and tried to help us memorize Psalm 23.

## Quarterman Street Grammar School

The month of August snuck away and was replaced by September strutting its stuff. The Waycross city schools were ready to open. Holding tight to Kathryn's hand, I gulped for air. I had a case of the heebie-jeebies, better known as being scared silly.

"Quarterman School is so big," I said. "I'm afraid I'll get lost."

Kathryn reassured me: "When school lets out each day, wait outside the door of your room for me. As soon as my teacher dismisses my class, I'll come for you. Remember: don't leave until I come."

Quarterman Street Grammar School was a brick structure with an unusual fire escape route. Once a month we had a fire drill. We'd line up single file under the guidance of our teacher, and one by one enter a circular tin silo attached to the main building. The silo was a gigantic slide that once we climbed inside, it sent us hurling forward until we landed on the ground. My first time going down the chute was frightening. Afterwards, since we never had a real fire hazard, going down the chute was loads of fun.

I hadn't been enrolled at Quarterman School long before my self-confidence took a nosedive. I felt like a waif wandering around in a crowded room of people.

My teacher kept trying to correct my penmanship, but my tiny hands couldn't cooperate. I lacked the finger dexterity needed for cursive writing, and soon both my teacher and I became exasperated. Cursive writing and I weren't jiving. Actually, more than my handwriting was on the skids. It's hard to feel good about yourself if others are creating perfect ovals and yours look like nervous balloons with the air seeping out.

When the school year ended, the principal and my teacher asked Mama and me to meet them for a conference. At the meeting they gave us the embarrassing news that I would not be promoted to the 4th grade. They attempted to soften the blow by reminding us that I had skipped a grade at Dixie Union School and was just now old enough to begin the 3rd grade.

I'm not sure I was old enough to understand their logic. It's difficult to estimate how being held back a year affected me. How many different ways can you label a loser? Stupid? Dumb? Washed-out? Being only 8 years old, my reasoning skills weren't fully developed. All I understood was that my classmates were being promoted—and I wasn't!

### Move #4

We didn't live on Alice Street long. Even when most people were still struggling to pay their bills, those owning rental property expected to be paid. If you got behind two months in paying your rent or utility bills, you were evicted—a fancy word meaning you had to either pay up or move.

We moved a few streets away to a small gray-frame house on Lee Avenue. The events that happened on Lee Avenue have deeply marked my life.

One day when Mama was working in the kitchen, I handed her a letter from my brother John. She stopped what she was doing and began reading the letter. Suddenly she cried out, "Harold, go to the dairy and tell Skeet to come home. I need him badly!"

In less than 20 minutes Skeet dashed into the kitchen. "Mama, what has you so upset?"

Mama handed him the letter. "Read this and you'll understand."

Skeet took the letter and began pacing back and forth as he read. When he got near the end of the letter, his visage changed. He tossed the letter on the bed and angrily exclaimed, "This letter makes my blood boil! Mama, this is John's way of telling you he can't help you pay the bills." Then Skeet turned on his heels and left abruptly.

I waited about 30 minutes before I sauntered into the bedroom and picked up the letter. The letter contained a sentence that I couldn't wrap my mind around. It went something like this, "From now on you should look upon me, not as your eldest son, but as your eldest daughter."

My brother John, a girl? That was about the silliest thing I could imagine. My childlike mind dismissed it as being impossible.

---

*I was a senior adult before I fully understood and appreciated John's courage and honesty. In the 1930s, to openly admit you were homosexual was tantamount to signing your death warrant!*

---

While living on Lee Avenue, another memorable event happened. Mama heard a knock on the door. When she opened the door, a postal worker said: "I have a big box addressed to Mrs. Cleo Sweat. It's very heavy. Where would you like for me to put it?"

Mama pointed to an open spot in the living room. The postal clerk set the box down and then left. All of us kids began pawing at the box like a pride of lions, anxious to discover its contents.

My brothers lost interest quickly when they saw that the box contained only smelly old books. When I had just about exhausted my search, my eyes fell on a familiar book. I clutched it to my breast and exclaimed, "Oh, Mama, look! This is the same Bible story book my teacher reads to us every day before we leave to come home."

Out of a big boxful of old books, only one book caught my fancy. Was it a happenstance that it was the same book my teacher was reading to our class every day? I don't think so. From that day forward as soon as school day ended, I'd rush home, find my copy of *Letters from Aunt Charlotte*, and read several stories.

Those Bible stories wrapped themselves around my heart and washed me with a special magnetic love. I found great comfort in the story about Jesus and the children. The disciples wanted to send the children away, but Jesus told them not to push them away—and not to get between them and him. Then Jesus gathered the children in his arms and blessed each of them saying, "Let them come to me."

I'll never forget the series of stories Aunt Charlotte wrote about the death and resurrection of Jesus. I cried when they beat him and hung him on a cross to die. Being only 7 or 8 years old, and with zero orthodoxy training, I nevertheless understood the simple truth: "Yes, Jesus loves me. Yes, Jesus loves me. Yes, Jesus loves me. The Bible tells me so."

Following Aunt Charlotte's suggestions, I quietly made my way to the back porch steps and told Jesus I loved him and needed him. Nothing overtly spectacular happened, but unknown to me that day as I reached up, Jesus reached down and embraced me in his arms of love.

Mama continued to be the stronghold in our family, and I felt more appreciation for her. On Mother's Day in May of 1939, I wrote her this letter:

Waycross, Georgia

Dear Mother,

How are you getting along? On this day of yours I hope you are happy. I hope you have a happy Mother's Day. I'll try to help you as much as I can. I'm glad you are living. I hope that J.W. (John) will get to come on Saturday, don't you? I hope we get to go to Grandfather's birthday. I am glad you have made my clothes for me. I hope you have a happy Mother's Day. I like my teacher. I thought about you when we were in the hall this morning: a girl sang a song about mothers.

Love,
Lynelle

## Move #5

Were you ever coaxed, against your better judgment, to take a ride on a Ferris wheel? Round and round the wheel whirls, only to suddenly stop with you suspended in midair. Your seat begins rocking back and forth and you die a thousand deaths, wondering if you'll survive. That's the way I felt about my family's being evicted from our rental property. The reason was always the same: we couldn't pay the rent!

Our house on Eads Street seemed larger than the houses we lived in on Alice Street and Lee Avenue. The house stood high above the ground, like our house in Haywood. A little girl my age lived next door to us. For the first time since moving to Waycross, I had a friend. I practically lived at her house. We played jackstones and fiddlesticks and sometimes played outdoor games such as hide-and-seek with her younger brother.

Good times often have a way of ending way too soon, though. The owners came demanding their rental money. We had no money with which to pay them, so we made plans to move.

## Move #6

From Eads Street we moved to State Line Road. The railroad tracks served as a dividing line. On one side of the tracks lived white renters like my family. On the other side of the tracks, in front us, lived a predominantly Black community.

My sister Kathryn struck up an acquaintance with some of the Black girls her age, and they began playing hide-and-seek together. Oblivious to color bias, Tunt enjoyed being with her new friends. Mama soon realized what was happening, though, and insisted that Tunt stop playing with her Black friends. Tunt implored, "I don't understand! Why can't we play together?" Mama shrugged her shoulders: "That's just the way it is: Black and white children don't play together."

*Looking back on Tunt's Black friends, I'm proud she attempted to break Georgia's cruel and stringent color barrier in 1938. None of us are born with racial blinders. Systemic racial bias has been growing by leaps and bounds, beginning with the American colonies' use of Africans as a means of slave labor.*

One afternoon my brother Skeet made a rare appearance at our house. He had with him a prized new possession: a green, plastic, battery-operated radio. "Mama, listen to this song everybody is singing." He turned the volume up high and situated the radio near the corner of a nearby table. We all perked up when someone began singing, "A-tisket, a-tasket, a red and yellow basket." When the singer came to the words, "trucking on the down the avenue without a single thing to do," Skeet twirled his right hand in the air, extended one finger, and strutted around the room. While Skeet was cavorting around the room, I accidentally touched the radio. The music ceased, and the radio's outer casing soon lay in splintered pieces on the floor.

As Christmas drew near, my motives for being on my best behavior were strictly mercenary. Kathryn and I were quite certain that John would send us a present, probably a doll. We wore Mama ragged trying to get her to tell us where our presents were hidden, but Mama held her ground. This called for some masterminded sleuthing! I didn't stop until I found the dolls, stashed away in a seldom-used clothes closet.

They bore a resemblance to baby dolls. However, dolls in 1938 were made mainly to be cuddled and to adorn a favorite spot on one's bed. That was fine with Kathryn, but not me! With my dolls, I was the mother and they were my children. Unfortunately, my dolls never held up under my constant nurturing. To make matters worse, when my new doll became tattered, I snuck into my sister's room and helped myself to her perfectly coiffed doll.

### Morton Avenue School

In the spring of 1938 a group of parents were planning Morton Avenue School's maypole dance festival. They were anxious for all of the students to participate. The girls were to wear white sandals and a white voile dress. Some of the parents had offered to buy me a pair of shoes if our teacher would find out my size.

I don't think my teacher intended to embarrass me, but when she drew off a copy of my bare foot in front of my classmates, my self-esteem dropped 10 notches. To compound the problem, several of the students snickered over my dilemma, making wisecracks about my poverty status.

Picking up on how humiliated I was over having my bare foot exposed before my entire class also hurt my entire family. I don't know where the money came from; I only know that before the time for the maypole dance, my family had bought me new shoes and a new dress!

The big day arrived. My partner was the son of the local Presbyterian minister. He was cute and courteous. If he minded being my partner, he never showed it. I recall us weaving in and out of the maypole streamers and doing a little dance step to the tune of "Skip to My Lou."

All is well that ends well, and the maypole dance was lots of fun in an otherwise disappointing school year. My teacher that year was tall, big-boned, and fat. One thing I liked about her was she enjoyed reading to us from *The Tales of Uncle Remus*. In my thoughts she is the same teacher who became dismayed as she tried to teach me cursive handwriting.

---

*Children growing up in a one-parent family, perhaps without realizing it, identify with the struggles of their mother. To have an authority figure treat their plight lightly is highly demeaning. The reverse is also true: Children instinctively know when a teacher is sensitive to individual needs and creates a climate of acceptance.*

---

### Move #7

Guess what? We moved again, this time to Kirkland Avenue, and I had to attend Isabella Street School.

At our new house we had an icebox made of wood that was approximately four feet tall. The upper fourth of the box was lined with tin, and that is where the ice man put our slab of ice. When the iceman stopped in front of our house, I dashed to where he parked his ice truck and watched as he chopped a 25-pound block of ice with his icepick. When he finished chopping the ice, he would grab it with large tongs and head toward our kitchen. While he deposited the ice in our icebox, I'd swipe leftover slivers of ice from the bed of his truck.

Occasionally one of Daddy's preacher friends would stop by to check on us. Usually, before they left, they would give me a nickel. I would race to the Hayloft, our local skating rink, and order a five-cent, double-dip, ice cream cone. When I got home, I would slice the cone down the middle and give half to my sister Tunt. Nothing could compare to a refreshing cone of ice cream on a hot summer day.

Tunt, now a budding pre-teen, often went to the Hayloft to skate and I would tag along—but I never skated. (I have no idea where she got the money to go skating: Perhaps one of her many boyfriends paid her entrance fee.)

### Gifts and Wisdom from John

In the South, if someone tells you about something that is so far away from anything you've ever heard of or imagined existing, you are prone to react by saying, "You don't say!"—which means, "You have to be kidding! There's no way that could be true." One happy day when John visited, I found myself saying just that.

We were squeaky clean and counting the minutes until John would arrive from Atlanta by train. We were anxious to hear about his recent trip to the faraway New York World's Fair of 1939.

When John walked up the steps to our house, Tunt, Herbert, and I grabbed him, practically sending him to the floor for one mighty hug. Nothing had changed materially. Our furnishings were still scant and our cupboard almost empty, and yet everything John said or did was like a magic potion.

Kathryn and Herb and I sat bug-eyed trying to understand what he was saying. The truth is, my brother was home and that was all that really mattered to me. Besides, New York seemed a million miles away from Waycross.

"Mama," John said, "it's a just a matter of time before you can get on a moving staircase of steps. Instead of climbing the stairs, you will just stand on the first step and the stairs start moving."

"The Lord have mercy!" exclaimed Mama. "What will they think of next?"

John laughed. "That's just the beginning! President Roosevelt spoke to us and, even though he wasn't where we were, we could both hear him and see him."

Mama shook her head. "I do declare."

John continued. "It's a little bit like

John Sweat

hearing his fireside chats from the radio, only with what they're calling television you both see him and hear what he's saying."

Mama rolled her big green eyes. "That fancy new machine is fine for New York and all those Yankee states. But I'm betting that if it ever catches on, only rich folk will be able to buy one. We certainly couldn't afford one."

John made yet another announcement: "Pretty soon, stores will begin selling a fabric called nylon. Already, ladies in New York are wearing nylon stockings. Also, they claim that soon electric typewriters will be sold. One company is promoting a handheld device called a View Master that allows people to see pictures of famous places. The View Master promises to become the poor man's way to travel abroad."

"How many people attended the fair?" asked Mama.

"More than six million were present for the opening of the fair."

"Glory be!" exclaimed Tunt. "I didn't know there were that many people in the whole world."

John pulled out a handful of small items from his suitcase and handed each of us something. He gave Mama items for Chandos and Harold.

I turned my tiny object around and around in my hands, trying to figure out what it was. I tugged on John's shirt sleeve and asked, "Is this a toy?"

"No, Ninkey. It isn't a toy. It's a tiny model of the big buildings at the World's Fair. The round building, called the Perisphere is 180 feet in diameter. Inside the dome of the Perisphere is a diorama telling us what the city of the future is going to look like. To get from the Perisphere to the Trylon, we took a ride on the world's longest escalator."

Herbert, who up until then hadn't opened his mouth, giggled before saying, "You meant to say elevator, didn't you?"

John ran his fingers through Herbert's curly hair. "Nope, we rode on an escalator."

Tunt raised her eyes and asked, "What's an escalator?"

John explained: "An escalator is like a moving sidewalk. You stand still and the escalator takes you to where you need to go."

Not wanting to be left out of the conversation, I inquired: "If I go outside and stand on our sidewalk, will it start moving?"

Ignoring my silly question, John squared his shoulders and reached over and gave Mama a kiss. "The real reason I came home this weekend was to wish Mama a happy Mother's Day." He then handed her a $10 bill and said, "I wish I could give you more."

Mama burst into tears. "Thank you so very much. I haven't told the children yet, but my work at the sewing room ends next week. I fear we're in for some tough times."

With the loss of Mama's job, our family finances reached an all-time low over the next few months. We depended a good bit on the redemption shopping center where we would cash in the wrappers of certain products to reduce the cost of items we wanted to purchase. As Christmas approached, I lingered in front of the redemption shopping center salivating over a Betsy Wetsy doll— and I made sure God, Santa, and Mama all knew what I wanted for Christmas.

When I opened my special Christmas package, though, my heart took a nosedive. John, who had gotten caught up in the national mania surrounding Atlanta's movie premiere of *Gone with the Wind*, had sent me a beautiful replica of Scarlett O'Hara. Where was my Betsy Wetsy doll? I flung the Scarlett O'Hara doll onto the bed and burst into tears.

*Although John always made me feel so special, the gift of the Scarlett O'Hara doll showed me that not even heroes are perfect. Some 50-plus years later in a San Francisco toy shop my eyes lit on a miniature replica of my Scarlett O'Hara Christmas memory. Today, that doll remains in a prominent place in my apartment year-round to remind me of the deep love I owe John. The oldest and youngest of Cleo and Ward's children were bound together with a love nothing could destroy. What as an elementary school student brought me great disappointment today floods my heart. The name John is another way of spelling Christmas.*

### Move #8

In 1940, when I was in the 4th grade at Isabella School and we were living on Kirkland Avenue, Mama lost her job with the WPA and we had to move again. She managed to rent a run-down house on Margaret Street in Old Nine, the most deprived community in Waycross but that figured strongly in the town's bygone days of rail supremacy.

Our new house consisted of three rooms with drop ceiling lights in each room. We had an outdoor privy.

It got so cold during the winter months that two of my brothers, now teenagers, took turns sneaking under our neighbors' house where they kept their stack of firewood. My brothers would grab a couple pieces of firewood and hightail it back home and quickly toss their stolen goods on the dying embers in our fireplace. After the neighbors raised a complaint, the boys broke some of our straight-back chairs and used them as firewood.

Although Mama was no longer employed with the WPA sewing project, we were still able to receive WPA food staples. When it came time to get our commodities, my oldest sister was too proud to show up in person at the distribution center but managed somehow to get our goods delivered to our house. The food boxes contained yellow grits, flour, a few oranges, and lots of grapefruit.

I recall receiving several one-piece cotton undergarments, too. The panty part consisted of rows across the top and three-quarters down each side, attached with tiny buttons and eyelets.

If a youngster like myself delayed going to the outhouse, it became nigh impossible to open your hatch soon enough to take care of business.

Our daily diet consisted mainly of fried potatoes, grits, biscuits, and fatback bacon. When a school cafeteria worker gave me a free meal ticket, following the example of my oldest sister, I purposefully lost mine in the girls' bathroom. The meal tickets for poor kids were green; those who paid for their lunch got a red ticket.

---

*By 1940, my family had moved eight times and I had attended several different schools. By anyone's standard, this period in my life was chaotic. To share it reminds me of someone hanging up their tattered rags for everyone to view. Despite all this, I knew I was loved by my family. My mother was an expert in spreading laughter during dire times, and I always welcomed her hugs.*

---

# 1940–1942

### Joe Millikin

After Mama's sewing center job with the WPA was terminated, how desperate, lonely, and forsaken she must have felt. Then she met a man named Joe Millikin, who had no marketable skills and probably only a grade school education, but at least he was working with WPA as a nightwatchman. This was better than having no job, but barely enough to pay the rent and feed himself and four girls. In addition, Joe could spin a yarn that had you believing everything was going to be alright if ....

For some reason, Mama sometimes took me along when she visited Joe. It probably had a lot to do with what was proper for a lady to do when calling on a possible suitor. At any rate, I distinctly remember being with the two of them in three instances.

The first encounter was late one afternoon at Joe's worksite. Joe was warming himself over an open pit fire. Mama and I sat down on the opposite side of the fire, and the two of them talked freely. There was no holding hands or kissing. I spent most of my time wondering why he had a big bald spot on the top of his head. Joe told me, "I have two girls about your age. Have your Mama bring you over to my house so we can all get to know each other better."

The second time involved Mama and me going to meet his children. The two youngest girls, Evelyn, better known as Cotton Top, and Thelma, perhaps a year younger than me, took to Mama's motherly ways like two puppies starved for affection. All I thought about was how much fun the three of us could have playing together.

The third occasion was when Joe took Mama and me for a ride in his rattletrap truck. He drove us to a wooded area surrounded by tall pines. There was no one else in sight. I never allowed the two of them to get further than 10 steps away from me. Thanks to me, whatever lovemaking Joe had anticipated never occurred!

I recall how Joe's eyes lit up when Mama told him that her property at The Sycamores was debt-free. She was probably thinking he would join her there and farm the land. (But I doubt if Joe ever did any hard labor in his entire life!) At any rate, the two of them were married by a justice of the peace in Pierce County on April 20, 1940.

---

*Only from my adult years spent with Mama can I begin to imagine the thoughts she might have had before her marriage to Joe. I don't believe she ever recovered from losing Daddy, the love of her life.*

*In my latter years I've asked myself questions about things that in my youth I took for granted: How many lonely hours did Mama spend as a single mom? How many times in the wee hours of the early morn did she live again the horrible news she got on July 19, 1931?*

*I find myself questioning the empty suggestions of her well-meaning friends and kin as they tried to satisfy the ache in her heart. "God needed him in heaven," was all our stunned friends could suggest as why an act of God had snatched our daddy from our midst.*

*I don't believe that God willfully and intentionally cut short the life span of John Ward Sweat Sr. Instead, I believe natural climate factors, such as lightning and gusts of wind, enhanced by two men standing in an open space, steered the flow of electricity to the nearest object of attraction, which unfortunately happened to be my daddy.*

*Even in her grief and forced poverty, she was determined to raise her children—all eight of us. To do this, she took on herculean homemaking skills using antiquated equipment. She cleaned the bare floors of our home with a heavy, corn-shuck scrub board and spent hours bent over an iron kettle steaming with homemade lye soap to clean dirty overalls and dresses. Mama kept her outdated Singer sewing machine humming to make us clothes. She fed us nourishing meals by canning fruits and vegetables in spring for our winter consumption.*

*Mama ventured forth to find a job when working for hire and getting a paycheck was something she'd never needed to do. She wrapped each of us in love and shared freely her gifts of storytelling and laughter while feeding our souls with her Christlike love. I can't remember Mama ever using profanity, imbibing alcohol, gossiping, or belittling others—even those she probably least liked.*

### Move #9

The next thing I remember is seven kids and two grown-ups scrambling to find a place to sleep in a long, narrow room filled with three double iron beds lined up with no vacant space between them. This left us with standing room only! There was a match-size kitchen attached to the long room.

Our living quarters, a former hotel, had dirty walls, dangling light fixtures, clogged plumbing fixtures, and lots of cockroaches. To take care of necessities, we traveled to the end of the hall where we had to share the facilities with other boarders, mainly unemployed adult males.

### Move #10

Six months after Mama and Joe married, we left our one-room apartment for a real house in Hebardville, beyond the city limits of Waycross.

I spent a lot of time in our backyard swinging high into the air on a tire swing, a homemade contraption made by tying an unusable automobile tire to a strong rope attached to the limb of a tree.

Someone told me that underneath where we lived was a land called China where thousands of yellow-skinned people with slanted eyes lived. That perked my attention! So, Herbert and I began digging to find China. I was so gullible that I expected to reach China any minute. After a week of extracting dirt, teaspoon by teaspoon, we finally gave up our quest.

I remember one time when we were living Hebardville that Mama got very mad. Joe's daughter Opal and my sister Kathryn were on the hot seat. They had managed, without telling Mama, to see their boyfriends in Waycross. Mama, visibly upset, gave both of them a physical and verbal lashing.

At yet another new school I felt like an unwanted stranger and didn't like my teacher. When she added my name to her attendance roll, she made what I perceived to be a snide remark about my family. I don't remember what she said; I only remember how, as child, I took it to be.

My Christmas gift from my brother John in 1940 was a metal table-and-chair set. I found that entertaining my make-believe friends there was more fun than attending school.

One day while waiting with my stepsisters for our school bus, I decided to turn around and go home. Mama never said a word about my returning home, but went about her usual cleaning chores.

Thinking she didn't mind that I had skipped school, I began entertaining my imaginary visitors with a party. After a while I grew tired and decided to come inside. At that point, lightning struck! As I sashayed through the arch connecting the living room to the dining room, Mama grabbed me and gave a thorough spanking.

Mama's arsenal of punishment tools included a hairbrush and the limbs extracted from a peach tree, with the peach tree switches by far the most painful.

But while troubles of an ordinary kind occasionally brewed between me and my siblings and Mama, matters were turning for the worse between Mama and Joe.

One day my brother Skeet came for a visit and to show off his new Ford Model T. He never said a word about Joe, but Mama knew that Skeet, like our brother John, did not approve of her marriage to Joe.

Soon, Joe's temporary job was on its last leg and he began sweet-talking Mama with a grandiose plan that unfortunately she believed.

"Cleo," he said, "If I just had a new truck, I could make it big selling produce in Jacksonville, Florida."

Mama frowned. "Why Jacksonville?"

Joe responded, "Four of my oldest children live in Jacksonville, and they tell me I could find a job there right away." Then he continued, "Honey, if you would take out a mortgage on your farm at Dixie Union, that would give me enough money to get a good truck." He hesitated. "You'll need to move back to your farm. I'll take Opal to live with her older sister Scotty; but Eretha, Evelyn, and Thelma need to stay with you. When I get settled and start drawing a check, I'll come and get you all."

Mama shook her head. "My brother Crawley will be angry if he hears I've put a mortgage on our farm."

"Why don't we keep the mortgage as our little secret? How about it, Cleo? Can I count on your help?"

Mama gave in and obtained a mortgage on our farm, and Joe bought a Ford truck with the money.

## Move #11

Before Joe left to make it "rich" in Jacksonville, in January of 1941, he moved Mama and Herbert and all of us girls back to RFD (Rural Federal Delivery), Route 1, better known as The Sycamores. For the Sweat children, it was like going back home. For the Millikin girls, it was uncharted territory. After attending three different schools in one year, I finished the 4th grade at Dixie Union.

Herbert was always looking for an excuse to miss school. If we failed to be ready to board the school bus at our house, we could walk down a dusty road for a mile and catch the bus as it began winding its way toward Dixie Union school.

On one bitterly cold day in February, Herb talked our stepsister Evelyn and me into joining him to play hooky. He said, "If you take baby steps, by the time you reach the crossroad, the bus will have already passed."

Throughout the day we romped over the countryside with Herbert as our guide, wading through icy water puddles and examining rocks that caught our fancy. As the day wore on, though, we began to worry about our fate once we made it home.

I think I remember this event so well because it coincided with my birthday. Mama was lying in wait for us when we returned home. I'm sure we got a few licks for playing hooky, but I soon forgot my punishment when Mama handed me a package and said, "This came in today's mail; it's addressed to you."

I opened the package quickly and found a book that John had sent me. The cover read Heidi by Johanna Spyri, and it showed a young girl holding on to the arm of an older woman who seemed to be taking her somewhere. Flipping through a few of the pages, I found Heidi talking with an old man. As soon as we finished eating supper, I began reading my new book.

---

*Today I understand that John was constantly seeking to expose my mind and heart to outlets of hope. To personally own a book was a rarity for me or for many other children in the South. Through our constant moves I had long since lost my copy of Aunt Charlotte's Bible Stories.*

*At times I also had access to books from a school library. I remember checking out Hans Brinker and the Silver Skates once. I readily identified with Peter and his sister Gretel, two very poor children, who both had a strong desire to win a skating contest. Yet Peter's desire to buy a pair of silver skates was postponed so his father could have surgery. Peter's unselfish action touched the heart of his father's doctor in a very special way, and the story had a heart-warming ending.*

---

### Move #12

Mama was wrestling with a problem with no easy solution. If she was to salvage her marriage to Joe Millikin, she could think of only one solution: leave Kathryn and me with Daddy's parents while she caught a bus to Jacksonville, hoping to find employment and a place to live. My sister Darcile, now employed as a grocery clerk at Jacksonville Beach, had agreed to help Mama find a job and a place to live.

While the transition was still in its formative stage, Tunt spoke vocally against the plan. "Mama, I don't want to spend my summer at The Forks of the Hurricane! Ninkey and I will be the only children within two miles of Grandma's house. We'll have to sit all day and listen to Grandma rant and rave about everybody and everything."

Tunt lost that argument. Mama went to Jacksonville, and Tunt and I wound up at The Forks of the Hurricane.

Early on I became fascinated with a deposit of damp red clay in a ditch across from Grandma's house. I spent hours molding plates, bowls, and animals. Afterwards I gave no thought to wiping my clay-caked hands on my dress. This artistic endeavor continued until my Aunt Annie, the family's unclaimed blessing, was busy washing the family's dirty clothes when she noticed the rising water was red. Dismayed, she called Grandma over to look at the red water. That ended my pottery project, but by no means did it cure me from my natural tendency to attract dirt like a thirsty dog on a muggy summer day. Dirt and I were good friends. On the other hand, Kathryn managed to run and play yet remain neat as a pin.

One evening when I must have looked like a rooting pig, Grandma took one look at me and said, "Stay right where you are: You can't come onto my porch with all that dirt." Someone handed me a bucket of water and after I washed away the grime, I was allowed to enter the screened back porch.

She adored Franklin Roosevelt, but despised his wife Eleanor for her association with Black people. Grandma was not shy about her hatred for this group and often used racial slurs in her comments about them.

Grandpa was a man with a generous smile. He didn't do a lot of talking, but when he did say something, everybody listened. His eyes twinkled, making you wonder if he had secrets he wasn't sharing.

Every night we gathered in Grandma and Grandpa's bedroom to witness Grandma's tobacco-spitting ritual. She'd ingest a plug of Bull Durham, and then in a little while from several feet away she'd let go a stream of tobacco juice onto the blazing hearth. This ritual must have impressed me a lot. Later, I'd put together a mixture of cocoa and sugar and pretend it was smokeless tobacco, and then place a wad of my concoction between my front teeth and lower lip. I finally gave up my habit as a lost cause.

But there were more important matters in the world than spitting tobacco juice. The war in Europe was getting worse. In the evening when Grandpa began fiddling with the dials on the radio, we all became deathly quiet. We knew war correspondent Edward R. Morrow was about to give us an update on the blitzkrieg, or "lightning warfare." Even a child could tell things were not looking well for our British friends.

## Release from Exile

The day came when Kathryn and I had about given up on hoping our situation would change. About that time a postcard arrived from Mama, saying she would be coming on Friday to take us back to The Sycamores.

Just before we went to bed on Monday night, Kathryn whispered to me, "I can't wait for Mama to get here so I can tell her all the bad things Grandma has said about her."

"If Grandma knew you were thinking of repeating the many times she said, 'Your Mama has forgotten all about the two of you,' she'd be fit to be tied."

Kathryn nodded. "Do you remember Grandma saying, 'Your Mama is too busy kissing her honey bun to think about you girls'?"

After the postcard arrived, Grandma was on her best behavior. One day she took me to the room next to the parlor and, reaching into the chest of drawers, pulled out a stick of peppermint. Handing it to me, she said, "I'm going to miss you when you leave on Friday. I won't have anyone to churn my cream into butter."

Daddy's brother Simon met Mama in Alma and brought her to the Forks. The way Grandma and Aunt Annie gushed and made a fuss over Mama, you would have thought they loved her dearly.

Finally, Tunt and I got some time alone with Mama. "You two are a sight for sore eyes!" she said. "I do believe you both are a foot taller than when I left for Jacksonville. I missed you so very much!"

"Mama," I asked, "Did you find a job and will we be moving to Jacksonville?"

Mama dropped her head. "No, I didn't find a job or a house. We're going back to The Sycamores, at least for the time being."

That's when Kathryn began spilling the beans, telling Mama all the bad things Grandma had said about her. Unbeknownst to Kathryn, Grandma was eavesdropping from the adjoining room and could hear every word that was being said.

All of sudden Grandma barged into the room. Her face flushed with anger, she charged toward Kathryn with a broomstick.

"Cleo," yelled Grandma, "Everything she's told you is a lie."

Glaring at Kathryn, Grandma screamed, "Take back what you just told your Mama or I'll beat you with this broom handle."

Mama stood up and put herself in front of Kathryn.

Peeking out from behind Mama, Tunt said, "No, Grandma. I will not take back what I told Mama. You are angry because you know it's the truth!"

Mama, who was known for never bad-mouthing anybody, said to Grandma, "Don't you dare hit my daughter with a broom stick. Thank you for taking care of my girls this summer. Excuse me, but we need to gather up their clothes. I think it's time for us to leave."

Thus ended our two-month exile. Grandma dropped the broom, and we made a speedy exit.

### Moves #13 and #14

We spent the remaining months of 1941 and the first half of 1942 at the Sycamores. Mama, John, Kathryn, and I then lived on Hicks Street in Waycross for a short time. Kathryn worked part-time as a long-distance telephone operator, and I enjoyed playing with my cousin who lived nearby.

At The Sycamores, electricity had been installed in 1940. Each of the rooms of our house had bulbs dangling from the ceiling by long drop cords. The light I couldn't resist turning off and on was encased in a large, round glass globe on our front porch. I felt like with a click of my fingers I could order the sun to appear. Mama scolded, "Lynelle, if you don't stop turning the light off and on, I'm going to have to spank you." That got my attention: at least I stopped until Mama was far away.

Now in the 5th grade, Mrs. Peacock, the principle's wife, was my teacher. I remember having two different desks that year. The first one sat on the left side of the room. One morning a mouse emerged from my inkwell, in a big hurry to escape. (To this day I have no use for mice or their relatives!) My second desk was located on the far right of the room. From that spot began the beginnings of my avid interest in American history. It seems that putting the past back together for viewing was something I relished in doing. I was in hog heaven when Mrs. Peacock said, "Get out your history book."

# My First Movie

If I'd listened to Mama, I'd still have my quarter. Furthermore, if I'd kept my mouth shut, I'd still have my quarter. Instead, I made sure everyone in my class knew I had a quarter and was on my way the following day to Waycross to see my first movie, *Snow White and the Seven Dwarfs.*

Grace King, a teenager, was the chief suspect. Grace had repeatedly been retained and often caught red-handed with coins and other items belonging to others. I'd left my quarter in the pocket of my coat when I went out to play Red Rover at recess. Grace didn't come out to play. When we returned from recess I searched for my quarter.

"My quarter is gone. Someone has stolen my quarter!" I yelled. "Now I won't get to see *Snow White.*" I was miserable for the rest of the school day and couldn't wait to get home and tell Mama what had happened.

Mama was sympathetic but said, "Ninkey, that's exactly why I urged you not to take your quarter to school today."

Tunt came to where I was sitting and handed me a dime. Herb handed me a nickel, and Mama managed to scrape together 10 pennies.

Tears trickled down my cheeks. "I have the bestest family in the whole wide world!" I exclaimed. I rushed over and hugged Tunt. Then I turned to Herb, but he pushed me aside and ordered, "Don't you go slobbering all over me."

The next day was Saturday. My cousin Charles came bright and early to pick Mama and me up in his new Ford with a retractable hood. He drove us to Aunt Estelle's house in Waycross. Mama and her sister had lots to talk about while my cousin Lonnette and I attended the matinee performance of *Snow White and the Seven Dwarfs* at the Ritz theater. It cost each of us nine cents to see the movie.

Charles came about 3:00 p.m. to take Mama and me back to The Sycamores where everybody was waiting to hear all about the movie.

"Ninkey-Stinky, did you like the movie, and did it make you wet in your pants?" asked Herb.

Tunt jumped in, "Was Snow White beautiful, and did she have a sweetheart?"

I caught my breath before beginning. "It's kind of hard to explain. I felt like I was no longer in my seat but in the room with Snow White, who was beautiful and loved by everyone except an ugly old witch. When the witch cackled, I held my breath. She was so angry over not being the fairest in the land that she tricked Snow White into eating a poisoned apple, which put Snow White into a deep sleep. Some tiny men then took Snow White to their house so they could take care of her."

Tunt pulled on my arm and asked, "Did Snow White have a boyfriend?"

I giggled before answering. "When the wicked witch put that spell on Snow White, we were told that only a handsome prince could awaken her. It seemed like forever before the handsome prince came riding up on his white stallion. He kissed Snow White and swept her into his arms and placed her on his horse, and they lived happily ever after!"

### Dining in Style

We always struggled to have enough money, and John was worried my siblings and I weren't getting a healthy lunch. Learning that Lott's Gas Station at Dixie Union provided hot lunches for the teachers, John set up an account with Lott's to provide lunch every day for Tunt, Herb, and me. We felt very special.

John clearly resented Joe Millikin's saddling Mama with taking care of his girls while he was living in Jacksonville, and did not provide lunch for Joe's girls. While they were dining on cold biscuits and slices of fatback bacon in lard buckets, we were enjoying hot roast beef sandwiches on store-bought bread, smothered in gravy, and fresh sliced tomatoes and snap beans.

### Red Flag Warnings!

Even before 1939, the headlines of the *Atlanta Journal* newspaper had warned of the rise of Nazism in Germany led by Adolph Hitler. As far back as my birth year in 1931, Germany had withdrawn from the League of Nations and German millionaires had thrown their support in favor of Hitler's emerging and powerful Nazi party. In 1932, Austrian-born Hitler received his German citizenship.

One year later Hitler was appointed as Germany's chancellor and granted dictatorial powers. His Nazi Party responded by starting the first concentration camp to exterminate all Jews from Germany.

By 1939, and in brutal fashion, the Nazis officially began boycotting all Jews in Germany. More than 60,000 artists, authors, painters, and musicians emigrated from Germany to countries that valued their presence.

I credit my brother John for keeping the windows of my mind open to the world where all sorts of things, good and bad, were occurring. He did so by providing us with a daily subscription to the *Atlanta Journal*.

One afternoon I glanced at the front page of the newspaper, where in four-inch letters Editor Ralph McGill warned of the German blitz befalling London, England. Every night hundreds of German planes were dropping bombs over the city. The article asked the question, "If London falls, will the Germans come to America next?"

Mama was troubled and got word to Uncle Simon, Daddy's brother, to come to The Sycamores. He came right away.

I remember the three of us—Uncle Simon, Mama, and me—standing near a cluster of pine trees. I listened as they talked. Mama asked, "Simon, what will we do if the Germans defeat England and come here?"

Uncle Simon's furrowed brow registered his anxiety. He threw his hands into the air and said, "Let's hope it never comes to that! The Germans usually bomb the big cities where thousands of people live. I suppose your best bet would be to hide in these woods."

Afterwards, in my dreams I found myself wildly running, trying desperately to dodge huge bombs exploding all around me.

### From the Halls of Montezuma

The postman delivered a telegram from my brother Harold, who was serving in the Marines. It read: "Come being sent overseas."

Mama began wringing her hands. "How can we go to Parris Island? We have no car, no money, and no driver!"

Located near Savannah, Parris Island was a long drive. When Skeet heard the news he said, "Mama, don't you remember Daddy's last words? Daddy said that where there is a will, a way will be made."

Mama sighed. "Okay, Skeet. Tell me your plan."

"Charles and I will find a car we can rent, and I'll call John and get him to send us money for the car rental and gas."

Up until this point Chandos had said nothing. He put his thumbs under his overalls bib and turned to Skeet. "Tell Mama about my driving."

"I know he's only 14," said Skeet, "but I promise you Chandos can get you to Parris Island and back home safely."

The following day we were ready to go. We loaded the trunk of the car with food and a tablecloth. Then Chandos, with no driver's license, crawled into the driver's seat. The rest of us—Mama, Darcile, Kathryn, Herbert, and me—scrambled to find a seat.

Five hours later we arrived at Parris Island and were met by armed military police asking who we had come to see.

"Private Harold Sweat, Sir," said Chandos.

In a few minutes the M.P. returned, saying, "Private Sweat is on his way. You may park your car."

Mama and Darcile got out of the car. Spreading out a large oil cloth, they began anchoring the cloth with fried chicken, tomatoes, corn on the cob, and a gallon of tea.

Before Mama and Darcille had finished getting the food out, Harold appeared looking spiffy in his Marine outfit.

"Glory be!" shouted Mama. "You're a sight for sore eyes!"

Harold wiped away the tears forming in his eyes and didn't stop until he'd got a good hug from everyone. After feasting on the homemade victuals, he said, "Mama, Aunt Tina's daughter Geneva lives in Savannah. Let's drive over there to see her."

We spent the rest of the evening in Savannah with my first cousin whom I had never met. Geneva said, "Aunt Cleo, we have a Sears and Roebuck store not far from here."

Mama was definitely excited. "Hush your mouth! Do you reckon we can go to the Sears and Roebuck store?" Then she threw her hands across her mouth. "Oh, my! I'm forgetting we promised to have the car back by tomorrow."

Geneva smiled. "That's no problem. My husband Aubrey will drive you and me to the store."

Mama nodded her approval. "John's been after me to buy some bags of chicken feed. I could buy a big bag of chicken feed and put it in the trunk of our rented car."

Aubrey added, "Aunt Cleo, if you want to stay with us and spend more time with Harold, I'll personally drive you to Waycross."

So, Mama stayed in Savannah. The rest of us, after another round of hugs from Harold and with the trunk of our car sagging from its heavy bag of chicken feed, left for Dixie Union.

It was close to midnight, and we were less than one mile from The Sycamores. We had crossed Thornton's Creek when we heard a loud booming sound. This was followed by a whooshing sound of escaping air. That sound was repeated not once but four times! We all managed to crawl out of the car to view a most pathetic sight. There sat our rented car with four very flat tires.

Darcile linked her left arm around Herb and her right arm around me while urging Chandos and Kathryn to latch on.

Darcile started walking toward home singing "I'll Fly Away," followed by one of Daddy's favorites, "I Shall Not Be Moved." Soon everyone was suggesting their favorite song. After we sang "What a Friend We Have in Jesus," I said, "Let's sing, 'Jesus Loves Me.'"

Through the creeping rays of early morn, Darcile spotted The Sycamores. "Look, everyone! In a few minutes we'll all be home."

I laid my head on Darcile's shoulder and muttered, "I'm tired as all get-out."

"Bless your heart, Ninkey. You were a real trooper. Let's get some sleep."

## December 7, 1941

Christmas, Halloween, and April Fool's Day are special days for most of us. Your birthday, on the other hand, is special because it marks the day you were born. There are other days, such as

December 7, 1941, that are known by millions of people because of
what happened on that day.

On that day I was 10—almost 11—and in the 5th grade. It was
a Sunday. We had spent the morning at Jordan Methodist church
and the preacher, Reverend Lee, had come home with us for dinner.
I don't remember what we had to eat that day, but the usual fare
when a preacher graced your table was to serve him fried chicken.
Chances are we would have also had hot biscuits and potato salad
and end up with a slice of Mama's burnt caramel cake.

As the day lengthened, we gathered in the living room close to
the hearth. While Mama and Reverend Lee chatted, I began tin-
kering with the radio. We all perked up when we heard First Lady
Eleanor Roosevelt say:

> I am speaking to you at a very serious moment in our his-
> tory. The Cabinet is convening, and the leaders in Congress are
> meeting with the president. The State Department and Army
> and Navy officials have been with the president all afternoon. In
> fact, the Japanese ambassador was talking to the president at
> the very time that Japan's airships were bombing our citizens
> in Hawaii and the Philippines and sinking one of our transports
> loaded with another on its way to Hawaii.

Reverend Lee, visibly moved by the surprising and alarming
words spoken by the First Lady, said, "There is no doubt in my
mind that tomorrow the U.S. will declare war on Japan.

I said, "I thought our enemy was Hitler and his Nazi airmen."

"Honey," said Reverend Lee, "Sooner or later we'll have to fight
not only Japan but also the Germans and Italians."

"The Lord have mercy," exclaimed Mama.

We didn't go to school the next day but stayed home to hear
Pres. Franklin Delano Roosevelt deliver a message to Congress and
the American people:

> Yesterday, December 7th, 1941—a date which will live in
> infamy—the United States of America was suddenly and delib-
> erately attacked by naval and air forces of the Empire of Japan.
>
> The United States was at peace with that nation and, at
> the solicitation of Japan, was still in conversation with its

government and its emperor looking toward the maintenance of peace in the Pacific.

Indeed, one hour after Japanese air squadrons had commenced bombing in the American island of Oahu, the Japanese ambassador to the United States and his colleague delivered to our Secretary of State a formal reply to a recent American message. And while this reply stated that it seemed useless to continue the existing diplomatic negotiations, it contained no threat or hint of war or of armed attack.

After President Roosevelt's address, Congress voted to declare war on Japan. The war declaration abandoned years of America's isolationist policy and ushered the United States into World War II. Within days, Germany and Italy—Japan's allies—declared war on the United States.

## The Axis of Evil

December 7, 1941 had been a long time coming. Germany, Italy, and Japan—the Axis of Evil—were lined up against the rest of the nations of the world.

German Dictator Adolph Hitler felt if he could get rid of all the Jews, the superior Aryan race would soon rule the world. Strange as it may seem, the Germans were well on their way to being victorious. The countries surrounding Germany, like stacked dominoes, were no match for Germany's Nazi tanks on land, nor its air power. Meanwhile, the United States looked on but did nothing to stop Adolph Hitler's insane antics.

In Italy, the Fascist Party under Dictator Benito Mussolini was also a far-right, authoritarian power. Italy freely used force to suppress anyone who defied the dictates of Mussolini or his black-shirted Fascist squads.

On May 22, 1939, Mussolini had signed a war pact with Germany. By 1940, Italy had declared war on France and Great Britain.

Far away from Germany and Italy, the island nation of Japan felt isolated and ignored from the rest of the world. Although it had fought with the United States in World War I, Japan came under American criticism for expanding its land holdings by attacking and capturing Chinese territory. The United States had particularly expressed displeasure with Japan's recent invasion of Manchuria and later its capture of Nanjing, a provincial capital city, where Japanese forces carried out six weeks of mass killings and rapes.

When the League of Nations condemned the Nanjing Massacre, Japan withdrew from the International League of Nations and in 1940 signed the Tripartite Pact, aligning the island nation with Germany and Italy. The union of the three principle Axis powers paved the way for Japan's sneak attack on Pearl Harbor on December 7, 1941.

And so, with 1941 drawing to a close, the U.S. and its allies were at war against three nations for whom brutality had no limits in warfare and the total decimation of their foes was the desired outcome.

---

*In my senior years I'm wondering if, because of its stringent enforcement of the Treaty of Versailles following the close of World War I, the United States helped stoke the fires of hate and blame that led to World War II.*

---

# 1942–1943

## Move #15

During the early days of World War II, my family moved to 705 Jackson Street in Jacksonville, Florida, and we entered our own combat zone. Hopeful of mending broken relationships amid hostilities, we wondered if our Humpty Dumpty of a family could be put back together again.

Jackson Street was only four blocks long. Two blocks north of our house was Riverside Drive, a much-traveled thoroughfare. After crossing Riverside from Jackson Street, we would be at the water's edge of the St. John's River, Florida's longest river. Our house was no better or worse than the houses we had occupied previously, with the exception being the seedy ex-hotel in Waycross.

About a half block south on Jackson Street was a community of Blacks. Many times I watched from my bedroom window as 50 or more gathered in an open area. Once my curiosity got the best of me, so I scooted down the sidewalk to eavesdrop on why such a large group of Blacks had gathered. From bits and pieces of their conversation, I soon understood that a Black man had been stabbed with an icepick by another Black person in their community. I didn't linger to hear anymore! I spun around and didn't stop running until I was back home.

There wasn't a house to the left or right of our dwelling. We occupied the downstairs portion of a dingy yellow clapboard house. We had to climb some steps attached to the rear to go upstairs. I only remember going upstairs one time. The sight I saw at that time still makes me feel queasy.

My stepsister Evelyn had a message for S.A., Joe's alcoholic son, and she talked me into going with her upstairs to his room. It was noon and S.A and his live-in companion Edith were still asleep on a dirty floor pallet. Edith wore an Aunt Jemina turban on her shaved head to rid herself of head lice. I breathed a sigh of relief when we got back downstairs.

### Chaos and Splintered Relationships

Since the death of Daddy in 1931, Mama had been the rock of our family. We looked to her for love and clung to her when hard times came calling. Our strong family ties began unraveling, though, after Mama married Joe Millikin. It had now reached a breaking point! At this time Herbert, 13, was living with our brother Skeet in Charleston, South Carolina. Darcile was living at Jacksonville Beach and employed as a cashier in a grocery store. Harold was serving in the Marines somewhere in the Pacific. Kathryn was scheduled to enroll in the 8th grade but declared, "I'm going to move to Orlando, Florida, and live with my friend Juanita Sears and her family."

I asked her, "What makes you think they will let you stay with them?"

Kathryn responded, "When the two of us were working at Bell Telephone Company in Waycross, we became good friends. Juanita was upset when her family moved to Orlando. She wrote and told me I'd always be welcomed to come and live with them. She also told me I'd have no problem getting a job as a telephone operator."

Meanwhile, the YMCA in Atlanta where John lived became the object of a police raid on homosexuals. John was among those fingerprinted and who spent a night in jail. The police, after filing a full report that included each of their names in the *Atlanta Journal*, turned them loose the next morning. John was so humiliated that he resigned from his job as an office clerk at Southern Railway and came home to The Sycamores. Later, his boss wrote a letter urging him to return to work. John did go back to work, but he wasn't there long before depression set in and he again returned to our farm. To compound his current frustration, he was now living in the same house with Joe Millikin, our stepfather, whom he despised!

One morning I woke up and discovered John had left home. He planned to hitchhike to The Forks of the Hurricane, believing our paternal grandparents would let him live with them. That left the Millikin girls, Mama, Joe, and me living at Jackson Street.

One memorable day Evelyn announced: "Mama, Daddy's being seeing the lady across the street from us and paying her money to have sex with him."

Mama, who believed her marriage vow to be sacred, shook her head. "You don't say. Honey, are you sure?"

"I saw him walk over to her house, and later he was sitting in a rocking chair on the upstairs porch. She was wearing a flimsy negligee and sitting in a rocker next to Daddy."

Turning red as a beet, Joe, in earshot of their conversation said, "Aw, Cleo, you know how it is. You weren't here and there she was, mine for the taking."

"That isn't the way I see it," said Mama. "You and I both promised we'd be married until one of us dies. Joe, I'm very disappointed in you!"

By the time of this unpleasant revelation, all of my siblings had left home—including Kathryn, who had moved to Orlando, and John, who hopefully had arrived at The Forks of the Hurricane. Could things possibly get any worse?

Grandma and Grandpa Sweat were troubled by the report that our first cousin A.C. shared with them about the police report in the *Atlanta Journal*, so they had Uncle Simon bring John back to Jacksonville that week.

While Uncle Simon was at our house, I eavesdropped on a conversation he and Mama had. Mama said to him, "Joe tells me that all men, at some time or another, have sex with another woman. You knew Ward quite well. Was he ever unfaithful to me?"

Uncle Simon grinned. "It's like this: I wasn't always strong in resisting loose women. However, you can be sure of one thing: Ward never, never betrayed his marriage vows to you!"

Uncle Simon soon departed for The Forks, leaving John more depressed than ever and Mama pondering if her marriage to Joe would last.

Back with us in Jacksonville, John busied himself by typing incoherent messages to someone unknown to me. The intended person he was writing to was someone John thought a great deal of and had betrayed him. John never finished one of those letters and wound up tearing them all into shreds.

Late one afternoon I heard John say, "My life is ruined. No one loves me. I'm going to drown myself in the St. John's River."

I told Mama what John had said and, not waiting for her to respond, I took off running to catch up with him as he marched toward the river, two blocks from our house.

Panting to catch my breath, I grabbed John's arm and pled with him, "Please, please don't drown yourself. I love you very much and would be brokenhearted if you should die."

John attempted to shove me aside, but I clung to him. After we crossed over Riverside Drive, all we could see was the murky, sprawling river.

I tried to convince John that such a death may be anything but peaceful. "Suppose you strangle as you go under? What if some sea creature begins eating you up while you're still alive?"

John seemed fixated on the many beautiful water lilies floating nearby.

When all else failed, I began to cry. That became more than John could handle. Ever so slowly he turned around and started walking back home.

Maybe Mama knew John would never take his own life. Maybe she didn't care—although I truly hope that's a wrong assumption. I don't remember her saying anything when we got back home, but I do recall that to my 11-year-old mind, John's suicide thoughts were a nightmare. It isn't any wonder I couldn't concentrate on schoolwork.

I did have two redeeming memories from the first time I lived on Jackson Street in 1942. On the front side of Riverside Avenue stood Faith Temple, an interdenominational church. One Sunday afternoon I decided to attend services there. No one would go with me, so I went alone. I sat down on a front row, to the left of the pulpit. The minister's message was simple and to the point. Sometime during the music and preaching I felt as if Jesus was wrapping his arms around me and whispering, "I know, I care, and I love you."

*This experience reminded me of the time when I was 7 years old and after reading about Jesus' death on the cross, I retired to the back porch steps and thanked Jesus for loving me so much. My second encounter with Jesus occurred in 1941, shortly after the outbreak of WWII. We were attending Jordan Methodist Church in Haywood, where my Aunt Belle was the church organist and my Uncle Crawley chaired the finance committee.*

*At that time, I was very afraid for what the future held for me and my country. I recall feeling that Jesus was inviting me to not be afraid. When I whispered to Mama that I was going forward to share with the congregation my decision to trust my future with Jesus, Mama employed one of her favorite controlling ploys: She pinched me real hard and said, "Don't do it; we're Baptists."*

*Thus ended my almost becoming a Methodist, but it did not end my feeling that Jesus was someone I could completely trust.*

### John Sweat, USMC

In mid-May of 1942 John returned home with a broad grin on his face. He gave Mama and me a snappy salute and said: "You're looking at a Marine. I stopped by the Marine recruitment booth a couple of hours ago. After chatting a few minutes, they asked me a few questions and gave me a brief physical exam. The Marine sergeant in charge said, 'Young man, your country needs you. Are you ready to become a Marine?' 'Yes, sir!' I answered. 'When do I report for boot camp?' Handing me an acceptance form to sign he said, 'Today is Tuesday. We'll get your orders ready. Report back here on Friday morning. We're sending you to Parris Island, South Carolina for boot camp.'"

At first neither Mama nor I could believe what John had told us. When it dawned on us that he'd been accepted as a Marine recruit, we were beside ourselves with joy. Mama said, "Glory be! You don't say."

John laughed and added, "Yes, Mama, I do say. I've listed you as my dependent. Once I finish boot camp, you'll start getting a check for $50 every month."

I began loudly singing "The Marines' Hymn," bearing down especially on the part about heaven's streets being guarded by the United States Marines.

Once John left for boot camp, we didn't hear from him for several weeks. Finally, a beautifully scripted letter arrived, filling us in on the rigors of combat training. Enclosed was a group picture, with John seemingly the epitome of health.

John completed his training satisfactorily and earned a marksmanship medal for his excellence in firearm shooting.

The last letter we received from him at Parris Island was full of what we considered to be good news. Along with a few of his Marine buddies, he'd been assigned to Washington, D.C. John had been chosen to be part of an honor guard that would be on hand when internationals would visit with President Roosevelt.

John's first guard appearance was when Queen Wilhelmina of the Netherlands made a state visit with FDR. She was a symbol of Dutch resistance to German occupation.

Suddenly we stopped getting letters from John. We didn't think it strange that we no longer heard from him; we assumed he was too busy to write.

## Move #16

Life at 705 Jackson Street in Jacksonville, it seemed, had only one way to go—and that was down. When Mama began getting a monthly check as John's dependent, she made a bold decision to leave Joe, who had long since lost the truck she mortgaged The Sycamores to buy. Now he had no job and wasn't even trying to find one.

When we got back to Waycross, I overheard Mama talking with the lady on Hicks Street we had rented from earlier. The lady reminded Mama she had left town owing her rent, but Mama promised "It will be different this time. I get a check once a month from the government as my son's dependent. I promise to pay you the back rent I owe."

The landlord relented and we moved into the same apartment we had briefly occupied earlier in 1942.

In September of 1942, I entered the 6ᵗʰ grade at William Heights Grammar School in Waycross, the most affluent grade school in the city. I desperately needed new shoes for school, as the soles of my only pair of shoes were threadbare and threatening to become disengaged at any moment. Shoes with rubber soles, though, were a highly rationed item during WWII.

Mama and I went to Calhoun's Department Store in the heart of Waycross. The shoe clerk, after measuring my foot, returned shaking his head and saying, "I don't have a pair of shoes in your child's size. The only pair I have is a half-size smaller than her foot measures, and I have no idea when we'll be getting any more shoe orders."

I tugged on Mama's arm. "Let me try them on. Maybe they'll fit."

After trying them on, I made a gallant effort to pretend the shoes felt fine, (I probably thought that if I didn't take that pair of shoes, I'd be shoeless for the rest of my life!) But my feet continued to expand, not shrink, and Mama became upset with me. I learned that pretending something is alright when it really isn't can get you into a heap of self-inflicted trouble.

At William Heights I may have been in the classroom with the richest kids in the city of Waycross, but my teacher Ms. Sue Snipes made an urchin like me feel accepted and welcome. After calling the attendance roll each morning, we sang a few patriotic songs such as "Remember Pearl Harbor" and "Praise the Lord and Pass the Ammunition."

Ms. Sue also read us a daily morning devotional. One of my favorites included this advice: "Be a bush if you can't be a tree. If you can't be a highway, just be the trail. If you can't be the sun, be a star. For it isn't by size that you win or fall. Be the best of what-ever you are."

In addition to my classroom education, I read many articles in the *Waycross Journal Herald* about the war. I learned that our government was sending more than 110,000 law-abiding Japanese Americans to live on the West Coast in internment camps. Their forced relocation occurred solely because they were Japanese, and we were at war with Japan.

Like most Georgians, I felt this action, endorsed by President Roosevelt, was justified. My response was no different than that of thousands of others. I reasoned that a Jap is a Jap wherever they live. A favorite saying in those days was "Remember Pearl Harbor!"

---

*Looking back, I understand how fear and racial hatred lay behind the forced internment of thousands of loyal Japanese Americans between 1942 and 1945. Today I see this as demeaning the basic citizenship rights of thousands of Americans solely on their racial identity.*

---

In January of 1943 Mama received a letter with some dreadful news: John was a patient at St. Elizabeth's Military Hospital for the Insane, and he was being discharged. Mama was urged to come and get him. She got in touch with Joe, and he agreed to go with her via train to get John.

When they returned with John I said, "This can't be my brother!" He was a stack of bones and contorted limbs. He wasn't responsive to any of us. The word "insane" sent shivers up and down my spine.

The next month, Mama decided to move us back to Jacksonville. I'm sure she must have felt she couldn't bear this burden alone and needed Joe's help.

### Move #17

In 1943 the sprawling city of Jacksonville with its Naval Air Station was a prime target for enemy infiltration. On a weekly basis bone-chilling sounds, emanating from air raid sirens, blasted the air waves. Each time the sirens wailed I thought *Is this alarm for real, or is it a practice drill?*

During the practice drills civilians wearing hard hats and beaming heavy-duty flashlights hither and yon routinely checked to see if every household had darkened their windows. After about 15 minutes the alarms ceased to sound, and the civilian volunteers left.

During this unsettled time, I finished the 6th grade in Jacksonville at Riverside Grammar School, built in 1917. The school, overlooking Riverside Park, was impressive with its Neoclassic columns and cornices.

I spent many happy hours on the swings and monkey bars at Riverside Park, an oasis of beauty and fun that offered me moments of freedom from my adult caring roles. Sometimes I played hopscotch with my stepsisters or watched the swans glide smoothly through the waters in their miniature lake.

My teacher at Riverside School, Miss Annie, whose size alone (about 200 pounds) I found intimidating, spent no time making me feel welcomed. She had moved to Jacksonville from Ohio when she was 18, and in that same year began teaching at Riverside.

Miss Annie was 72 and her appearance can best be described as dowdy. Her hair was silver, and she wore oxford shoes and seemed to walk with a slight limp. I can't remember her ever laughing or even smiling: she was a strict disciplinarian. It was obvious to all of us that two girls were her pets. These two girls were impeccably dressed, always turned in their homework, and knew the answers to every question.

Near the end of the school year in May, Miss Annie got in touch with Mama and told her I needed a white dress to wear for our graduation service commemorating our passage from grammar school to junior high. Mama assured her she'd get me a white dress. Spiffy in my new white dress, I "graduated" from grammar school—actually, my passing the 6th grade was an act of mercy, not merit.

## My Woes Multiply

I was ill-prepared for junior high school. At John Gorie School in Jacksonville, the classes were huge, and instead of having one teacher I had at least four. I felt like I was simply a number with no meaningful contact with my teachers or classmates. I was lonely and preoccupied with the rollercoaster ups and downs associated with John's recovery. The visible demonstration of my inner frustrations became most obvious in my handwriting.

My school gave great emphasis on buying war saving stamps. Each of us was given a savings stamp booklet. Each stamp sold for 25 cents and when we had purchased 75 stamps, our booklet was full and worth $18.75. We could then redeem it for a $25 war savings bond after 10 years.

I felt like a first-class heel when most of the kids in my class, except me, were buying savings stamps. If my teachers and classmates had known how much it hurt and embarrassed me that I couldn't participate in aiding our war effort, perhaps they wouldn't have stared so hard at me when my name was called.

All my efforts at home to help win the war didn't pan out. I scrounged the neighborhood without any luck, hoping to find some scrap iron or even an old tire. I traced off a large V in my backyard for a "victory garden," hoping to grow some vegetables, but my effort was in vain. I began hoeing away, only to discover that the only site available was loaded with rocks and weeds. The exposed patches of dirt were few and far between. As if that were not bad enough, soon I found myself in another embarrassing situation.

One day my 7th grade music teacher played a scale on her piano, asking each of us to individually repeat the note she sang to us. When it came my turn, I was petrified. I was the only girl out of 12 she labeled as alto, causing some of the boys to snicker. As far as I was concerned, my music teacher might as well have announced to the world that, like my brother John, I was "different!"

---

*It's important for parents and teachers to discover the way children see themselves. There were lots of innocents in my choral vignette. The music teacher was assuming a natural role by getting us ready so she could assign us parts to match our voices. She had no way of knowing all that was happening with my brother John. Having some of the boys laugh at my being the only alto diminished my view of myself even more.*

*I was spending lots of time trying to figure out who I was. Unfortunately, for me, no one in a position of authority considered my needs as being significant. It is good to remember how a child perceives herself. Whether the feelings are real—or in my case imagined—self-perception is of vital importance.*

---

### My Hero Is Insane!

Through the centuries, insanity labels have brought about a mixed bag of reactions—many of them cruel, destructive, and seldom helpful. Mental issues within a family too often have been a hush-hush topic. Family members somehow believe the problem will correct itself. Instead, silence usually magnifies the problem.

The Marine Corps personnel in charge of veterans in Duvall County contacted Mama with an offer to give John electroshock treatments in a private sanatorium on Trout River, some five miles away from our house on Jackson Street. The letter explained that John would spend seven weeks in the sanatorium with no visits from the family for the first three weeks of his treatments.

Feeling desperate and believing there were no other options available, Mama accepted the veterans' worker's recommendation for shock treatments.

Nationally, these treatments had become a huge success in 1943, particularly among WWII veterans who had depression or schizophrenia. Treatments usually began prior to breakfast, with the patient being given anesthesia and a muscle relaxant before two electrodes were attached to the scalp. This was followed by applying electric current to the electrodes, resulting in the patient having a brief convulsion.

In late October, John was eligible to receive visitors. It was close to Halloween when I got on a city bus, wearing my gypsy outfit. I dropped my five-cent coin into the token box and shared with the bus driver John's new address. When I got to the sanatorium, someone escorted me to John's private room.

John met me with a wide grin. "Hello, Ninkey. It's so good to see you!"

After a grand old hugging session, we settled down to talk. John seemed physically fit and mentally alert. Wanting to do something tangible, I offered to buy the two of us a Coca-Cola, not thinking I had to save enough money for the transit ride back home.

When it came time for me to leave, I reached into my change purse, scrambling to find a nickel, but came up emptyhanded. What I should have done and what I did at that point are vastly different matters. Instead of asking someone for five cents or explaining my predicament to the bus driver, I started walking. (I guess I thought the bus driver would turn me away, and lately I'd had more than my share of rejections. Children can handle just so many put-downs before they start seeing themselves as rejects.)

Still in my gypsy outfit I walked, and I walked, and I walked! Finally, as shades of night began creeping over the city, I spied a sign that read "Jacksonville City Limits." I expelled a feeble but grateful sigh. About 30 minutes later I was back home, giving Mama a glowing report on John's progress.

## D-I-V-O-R-C-E

Meanwhile, Mama began secretly talking with her sister Maude. I accompanied Mama to the local neighborhood grocery store in Jacksonville to use a pay phone. While Mama dropped coins into the machine to continue her lengthy conversations, I never left her side.

The first thing Mama shared with Aunt Maude was that she planned to divorce Joe. Mama believed in the marriage vow, "until death do us part," but she had hung on to a fabricated union way too long. My aunt, who was an active member of Central Baptist Church in Waycross, gave Mama a wellspring of hope by assuring her that she was making the right decision. She buttressed Mama's hope that she had biblical grounds for ending her marriage.

---

*The divorce rate among Americans in the early 1940s was only 2 per 1,000 people. Grown-ups, when talking about a failed marriage, quoted the adage, "If you make your bed hard, just lie in it." This generally meant, "If your marriage fails, do nothing to end it. You should remain with your spouse and suffer the consequences."*

---

With her first decision finalized, Mama's life became more complicated: Mama wanted to pay off the mortgage she had put on the farm, sell the farm, and buy a house in Waycross with rooms she could rent for additional income. There is no telling how many weeks were involved in bringing this project to fruition. I feel reasonably sure Aunt Maude worked with my Uncle Crawley and local realtors to find the best possible house for us.

It was a proud day for Aunt Maude, Mama, and me when all that was left for Mama to do was to sign her name on the legal papers. At that moment, even as a child, I knew Mama's decision to divorce Joe and to buy a house in Waycross proved she was a woman determined to rise from the ashes of defeat and to forge new paths. Thus, a vital part of my inheritance is having a Mama who refused to remain in a failed marriage and wasn't ashamed to call on her trusted sister for help. Mama sought change instead of despair.

---

*I believe it demonstrates courage when we own up to our personal errors. However, admitting our wrongs is simply the first step. Whenever possible we must follow through with specific actions that bolster our intent. For example, I now realize I have been party to a culture that espouses systemic racial views.*

*I'm convinced that racism has been part of my entire life and, while I've done more than many people to bring about racial justice, I'm acutely aware that I must do more. I need to borrow some "Mama courage."*

---

Shortly before exiting John Gorie Junior High School to return to Waycross, I did something I'd been wanting all year to do. Plopping down four shiny quarters on the top of my desk I said, "Mrs. Black, give me four saving stamps." When I looked up, my eyes fell on a sea of smiling faces.

---

*The time I spent at 705 Jackson Street in 1942 and again in 1943 reminds me of someone meandering through a tricky labyrinth. Even today this portion of my life is a basket of painful memories with parts of the timing still murky. But that time is also a part of my inheritance, even if I'd rather not claim it!*

---

### Move #18

In Waycross our new home on Lincoln Street ran parallel with Hicks Street. If I cut through my neighbor's yard, I could be at Aunt Estelle's house in three minutes or less. I was excited over the prospects of renewing my friendship with my cousin, Lonnette. In 1942, before we moved a second time to Jacksonville, I had spent many happy hours traipsing down Hicks Street to her house to play Monopoly.

Mama's sisters, who in my early years showered my family with loving support, were waiting at our new house when we arrived in Uncle Simon's truck. My aunts had sandwiches and iced tea ready for our consumption.

Our new wood-frame house was light gray with white trim. A porch spanned three-fourths of the lower and upper portion of the house. A long hallway extended from the front door to an enclosed back porch. On the left were a bathroom and a very large room. On the right side of the hall were three rooms, the last being our kitchen. Mama and I occupied the room next to the bathroom, and John had the front bedroom on the right side of the hall. (The upstairs floor plan probably matched our downstairs layout, but I only remember being upstairs on one occasion. When my sister-in-law, Doris, gave birth to my second niece, Diane, Skeet brought Carolyn, their oldest child, to stay momentarily with us. Carolyn cried nonstop, begging for her mother!)

There were many houses on the same side of the street as ours, but only one house stood on the opposite side of our street. Close to it was an underpass built to accommodate the passing trains above. Below, drivers and passengers in cars, bicyclists, and pedestrians traveled along Plant Avenue, the main downtown artery of Waycross.

To the left of our house was a huge, undeveloped lot. At the end of our one-block street going north, was a massive array of train tracks, with locomotives belching out flying cinders and tons of smoke.

As usual, we experienced both the good and bad—and the in-between. On the brighter side, Kathryn returned home and was rehired by Bell Telephone Company, and Mama and I began attending Central Baptist Church with Aunt Maude.

On Dec. 6, 1943, I enrolled in the 7th grade at Waycross Junior High. I got excited when I heard I'd be taking a course in American history. However, my history teacher's test questions did me in. They went something like this: The _____ _____ in 1848 was an example of _____. Despite receiving consistent C's on my report card, nothing diminished my thirst to learn of our country's early beginnings.

Other subjects interested me less. One day my English teacher summoned me to her desk and shared with me that she remembered reading about my daddy's death in the *Waycross Journal Herald*. I thought it was kind of her to share that information with me. It made me try harder to keep my mind on subjects, verbs, and their tenses.

Meanwhile, at home my brother John continued to withdraw from the real world. His condition got worse instead of better. His future appeared bleak.

---

*The glowing results of John's electroshock treatments at the Trout River sanatorium evaporated in less than two months after he returned home. The tragedy attached to these treatments is now clear to me: John was gay, and being a homosexual in the United States in 1943 was totally unacceptable. No one in the arena of medicine or religion was advocating that it was normal to be gay.*

*Shamefully I must admit that even as a freshman in college I was still writing to John telling him that all he had to do was repent of his sin and that God would forgive him. Mama said that when John's social worker read my letter, she exploded with anger and told Mama, "How dare your daughter set herself up as knowing what is and isn't a sin!" This happened when John was on an open ward at Linwood Veterans Hospital in Augusta, and enjoying going to dances and participating in theatrical productions.*

*Shame on me! Double shame on the religious leaders, politicians, and medical professionals whose biased views held sway.*

*John's social worker served as a beam of light, pushing a taboo subject forward and demanding that psychologists and family members take a new look at a centuries-old problem.*

*The American Psychological Association in 1975 took a bold stand by declaring that being gay is normal, and then declassifying homosexuality as being deviant.*

---

# 1943–1945

## My First Job

After Kathryn returned to Waycross, she encouraged me to seek a job at the Plant Avenue Rexall Drug Store during Christmas break. I talked with the store manager about working in the sandwich shop, and he hired me. My main job was to wash the thin Coca-Cola glasses. Not a day went by without me nursing several cuts on my hands. (Obviously, child labor laws, if they existed, weren't enforced: I was 12.)

One afternoon a train loaded with U.S. Army troops stopped at our Atlantic Coastline station to give the soldiers time to get a bite to eat. About 20 of them made their way to our fountain and began ordering sandwiches and Cokes. Our head waitress looked over the crowd. Seeing that one of the soldiers was Black, she almost fainted. Flustered and not knowing what to do, she rushed to counsel with the store manager. Wisely, the manager insisted she take the soldier's order. Biting her lower lip, she did so—but later uttered some choice racist comments.

When I received my first paycheck for one week of work, I went straight to Churchill's Merchandise Store that dealt exclusively in selling dry goods. I picked out a bright, tartan wool piece of material, and the clerk helped me select a pattern for a skirt. After my purchase was complete, the store had a unique way of finishing the order. My material and pattern were placed in a wire basket, and my signed check was encased in a tube. A pulley transported my purchase to an upper level where someone handled the money transaction.

Whatever was left of my check I turned over to Mama to help buy groceries.

## Making Our Way Forward

In 1942 the U.S. Army Air Forces had leased 3,000 acres from the city of Waycross and constructed an airport. By August of that year Waycross Army Airfield was activated as a sub-base of Hunter Army Airfield in Savannah. The base in Waycross at first was far from being completed, so the facility was utilized as a tent city.

By the time of our arrival in Waycross, the 499th squadron had returned to Waycross and the main activity for the base had turned to training fighter-bomber replacement pilots by the 501st Fighter-Bomber Squadron.

Although the Air Force offered many amenities, many military families preferred to live off base. A couple from Michigan rented our upstairs furnished apartment. The wife had flaming red hair and bonded easily with Mama. The couple also had a precious little toddler named Sue who I sometimes babysat with for 25 cents.

Mama's caring for young adults far away from home was deeply appreciated. She excelled in fixing up an apartment and keeping the rental fee low. Soldiers and their families took to Mama's kind, gentle ways.

While my academic grades faltered, I was adept at pulling on the heartstrings of my siblings. To my brother Harold, a Marine serving in the South Pacific who had written of his good luck in gambling, I wrote, "I'd love to join the Girl Scouts, but buying a uniform is costly." Several weeks later a check for $50 arrived in an envelope addressed to me. By then I'd changed my scout plans in favor of buying a bicycle. From that day forward I could be seen weaving in and out of the streets and alleys of Waycross on my bike.

I wasn't the only one attracted to my bicycle. One morning John slid into a white uniform he found hanging on the clothesline. The dress belonged to the lady living in our upstairs apartment. John took off on a bicycle joy ride up and down Lincoln Street. Mama, Kathryn, and I were mortified! We died a thousand deaths until he returned home, hung the white uniform back on the line, and spent the rest of his day and evening sequestered in his bedroom.

That same day our pastor, Durwood Cason, came for a visit. I listened as Mama shared with him about John's joy ride. He waited a little while before speaking. Dr. Cason's response was laced with love for John and for each of us.

### Mama's Driving Lesson

My brother Chandos, who I hadn't seen in more than four years, drove from Portsmouth, Virginia, to check on us and to see our new house. He was driving an old Dodge car.

During WWII, if you drove a car, you most likely were driving an older model because the automobile companies stopped making cars and concentrated on making only military equipment. Tires, even old ones, were hard to come by. A used car could be purchased for as little as $500. Chandos, who now preferred being called C.D—short for Chandos David—insisted Mama try her hand at driving. After much cajoling, she agreed. I raced to the phone and called Aunt Estelle, telling her to be on the lookout for us.

C.D. slid over to the vacant passenger seat, and Mama climbed into the driver's seat. I hopped into the back seat, poised to witness Mama's maiden lesson.

C.D. explained how to start the car and that Mama needed to always keep her hands on the steering wheel. The starter was located on the floor of the car. C.D. backed the car out of the driveway and then said, "Mama, we're now in your hands."

Everything was going well until we were directly in front of Aunt Estelle's house. Mama, determined that her sister Estelle saw her driving a car, forgot all about keeping her hands on the steering wheel. She waved furiously as we approached Estelle's house.

It's a good thing no cars were coming from the opposite side of the street. When Mama took her hands off the steering wheel to wave, the car veered to the opposite side of the road.

C.D. shook his head. "Mama, remember: never take your hands off the steering wheel when you're driving."

This concluded Mama's first and last driving lesson. She never got behind the wheel of a car again. (But in her senior years she became an expert backseat driver!)

## Visitors From Jacksonville

In early March of 1943 one of Joe Millikin's daughters brought Joe by our house with a peace offering. Just seeing him standing in our yard angered me. I was like a bantam rooster protecting her turf from a rooster four times her size. I screamed, "Mama has divorced you. You are not welcomed here!"

Mama took over. "Joe, why have you come?"

Joe held up a tiny jewelry box. "I promised you a ring when we got married, and I never kept my promise."

Mama said, "I'm sorry, Joe. I can't take a ring from you. Our marriage is over."

Joe said, "Please take the ring. I want you to have it. You don't have to worry about seeing me anymore."

Mama went down the steps where he was standing on the ground. He handed her the jewelry box and mumbled a husky goodbye.

About a month later, on a Saturday night, there was a knock on our front door. When I opened the door, I saw five very familiar faces. Opal and her Navy husband Robbie, Eretha, Evelyn, and Thelma rushed in and gave Mama a great big hug. Their visit turned into a mini homecoming. They came to tell her how much they loved her and that they didn't blame her for divorcing their daddy. We rehashed lots of happy memories. After an hour or so of visiting, Joe's girls returned to Jacksonville.

Their visit, so spontaneous and loving, meant much to Kathryn and me and especially to Mama. It demonstrated in a tangible way the deep respect and love that Joe's girls had for Mama. She had filled a big void in their life, and they were grateful.

Never again did I see or hear a word from Joe Millikin or his daughters. But I can't erase the four years of my inheritance I spent in Mama's on-and-off relationship with that man.

Meanwhile, I was going through puberty with high and low emotional outbursts. The world war also raged on.

## My Faith Home

Finding a spiritual home during my teens reminds me of a man panning for gold. When he strikes a gold vein, he often shouts, "Eureka!"

Acceptance in my house of faith ranks at the top of those things I have inherited. For weeks on end my cousin Lonnette and I occupied a place on one of the front middle pews at Central Baptist Church. This section of the church was reserved for children only.

The only Bible either Lonnette or I owned was a red-lettered pocket edition of the New Testament, distributed by the Gideons, an international Christian businessmen's group.

On an Easter Sunday in 1943, Lonnette and I came ready to tell the entire church body we wanted to become Christians. As soon as Brother Cason stepped down from the pulpit to give an invitation, the choir began singing "Jesus Paid It All."

A long line of people came by to congratulate us on the decision each of us had made. When Mrs. Carswell, one of the choir ladies, hugged me I told her, "I wish the choir had sung, 'Just as I Am.' She responded, "Someday you'll love 'Jesus Paid It All' just as much as you now love 'Just as I Am.'

Lonnette's parents weren't active in any church at the time, although Aunt Estelle's parents, especially her mother, raised all her children in the Methodist faith.

Lynelle, age 13

The rite of baptism was a sacred moment for me. It seemed to solidify, in a beautiful and meaningful way, my commitment to follow Jesus. I probably envisioned myself rising from the baptismal waters to sin no more. Alas, it wasn't long before I reverted to using profanity and throwing temper tantrums. I was a neophyte Christian. Evidently my tongue didn't get baptized!

*What I understand now but did not understand then is that I'll always be a neophyte Christian. Hopefully, I will forever be in the process of becoming a Christian.*

Many years later Aunt Estelle showed me Lonnette's Gideon Bible where she had scribbled, "If this Bible is lost, please contact my nearest of kin, Lynelle Sweat."

## World War II

In 1943–1944 the war in Europe began to favor the Allies when the German and Italian forces surrendered North Africa to the Allies. This was followed by the overthrow of Italy's dictator Benito Mussolini. Italy in turn declared war on Germany—only to have a long, hard battle before they could depose of Nazi Germany's puppet ruler.

The battle for Stalingrad, Russia, after a cruel and devastating conflict, ended with the official surrender of Germany's 6th Army to Russia.

Back home the war effort brought profound changes such as the number of women in the workforce and the increased rationing of certain items.

The U.S. Department of Labor Bureau's Statistics indicate that before WWII, women who worked outside the home usually did so in jobs considered "women's work" such as teaching, clerical work, nursing, and library science. By 1944, women held a third of all the manufacturing jobs in the U.S.

During the war, women took on jobs formerly held by men who were serving in the U.S. armed services. Unfortunately, the women worked for lower pay. And after the war, the jobs held by women were turned over to the soldiers returning from the battlefields.

*In 1944 the average female skilled worker earned $31.21 a week, while the average skilled male earned $54.66 a week. It saddens me that more than three-quarters of a century have passed since the end of WWII and women are still paid less than their male counterparts. There's also a high differential between what white women earn and*

*Black women earn. I guess a good prayer would go like this, "Dear Lord, please save me from being born a female and especially as a Black or Latina female!" (pun intended).*

In addition to transforming the role of women in the workplace, the war dramatically altered American's shopping options. Shortly after the U.S. went to war against Japan and Germany, the federal government created a system of rationing to limit the amount of goods a person could buy.

The Office of Price Administration, established in August 1941 to control war-time prices, initiated the rationing program in late 1942 to support the war effort. Soon many products once taken for granted by many Americans became difficult, if not impossible, to obtain, including bacon, butter, beef, bubblegum, sugar, to shoes, automobiles, tires, gasoline, fuel oil, coal, firewood, nylons, silk, and shoes. Rationing cards that limited quantities of various commodities were first issued to the American public in May of 1942.

In February of 1944 tokens debuted, furthering restrictions on consumer purchases. Most Americans accepted the restrictions freely, but as in any crisis in which a government restricts the flow of goods—Prohibition being an earlier and notable example in the United States—the authorities had to contend with a thriving black market where scarce goods could be obtained illegally.

During this time of shortages Mama often sent me to the grocery store with tokens to purchase spices, black pepper, beef, and sugar. Sometimes the store would already be sold out of the items we needed.

While we managed the best we could, in the summer of 1943, Mama and her sisters gathered at Aunt Minnie's house to celebrate the medical discharge from the Marines of Minnie's son Twyman Jr., who had fought the Japanese in the Battle of Guadalcanal. He'd lost lots of weight and looked as if he were to encounter a strong gush of wind, he'd never survive. I sat spellbound next to him on my Aunt Minnie's porch as he shared with a group of us the horrible atrocities he had seen.

Twyman said that the "Japanese soldiers were disciplined and vicious. When a Jap captured a Marine, they cut off his head with a saber and then stuffed some of his body parts into his mouth. If a Marine ever escaped from a Japanese soldier, the Jap would take his own life. After our k-rations gave out, we had to scrounge for food. At one point all I had to eat was Japanese rice and oats that were crawling with maggots and worms."

I interrupted Twyman and asked, "Where is this place you call Guadalcanal, and why was it so important?"

Twyman shuddered and let go a heavy sigh. "Guadalcanal," he said, "is northeast of Australia and it is a tiny jungle island in the southwest Pacific Ocean. Our task was to capture a major air base belonging to the Japs at Rabaul."

Someone else asked, "How long did the battle last, and did the Marines win?"

"My Marine unit landed on Guadalcanal on August 8, and it took us and our Allies almost seven months before the battle was over." Twyman wiped away the tears flowing down his cheeks before saying, "The island was steamy hot, and it had a nauseating odor that made many of us sick. We were bombarded by mosquitoes."

---

*At least 60,000 Marines and soldiers died, and the Japanese lost 31,000 men during the Guadalcanal campaign. The U.S. also lost 29 ships and 615 aircraft. The Japanese lost 38 ships and 683 aircraft. The Battle for Guadalcanal began on Aug. 7, 1942, and ended on Feb. 9, 1943, with a victory for the Allied forces. This constituted the first major Allied victory in the Pacific Theater of Operations.*

---

To this day, when I recall my cousin's emaciated body, I still get goosebumps. General Sherman during the American Civil War is quoted as saying, "War is hell." I tend to agree with Sherman.

Meanwhile, on Lincoln Street, John threatened Kathryn and me with a butcher knife. Mama realized something drastic had to be done.

### A Gut-Wrenching Decision

Mama's heart was heavy when she asked the telephone operator to connect her to the veterans' hospital in Augusta. When the connection went through, Mama asked to speak to the person in charge of taking in new patients.

The man in charge first asked Mama a lot of questions concerning John's legal status, and then waited for Mama to share John's specific actions of late. It was decided the hospital would send two interns to pick John up and escort him to the hospital.

Two guys arrived around 10:00 a.m. the next day. John slipped into his clothes and went with them without a murmur. One of the interns lingered behind to inform Mama about visitation rights and told her someone would be in touch with her shortly about his room assignment, etc.

When the car with John in it left our driveway, I ran to Mama's open arms, tears cascading down both our cheeks.

Mama said, "I didn't know what else to do. Do you suppose he'll ever forgive me?"

I whispered, "I know Mama, I know Mama. I'll go with you to see John soon."

## Teenage Memories

My 8th grade science class was taught by an unclaimed blessing named Bessie Maynor. Miss Bessie was built like a heavy-duty tractor, and she allowed no nonsense from her pupils. If only I had bothered to read my text assignments, I might have enjoyed her class. Instead, I lived in mortal fear that she would ask me a question.

During this time my Uncle Andrew Jordan died, and John's vacant room served as his lying-in-state wake. I and some of my younger cousins stayed up all night with the body. (This was the only time in my life when I was part of a wake service, as the ritual soon started fading away.)

My first cousin Anna Bell Rowland and her friend Delores, cashier employees of the new Big Star supermarket, soon rented John's room. Mama added the perk of allowing them to use the kitchen for free. During their stay with us I was an absolute first-class nerd. I practically lived in their apartment, barging in unannounced and forever overstaying my welcome.

I remember going only once with Mama to visit John in Augusta. I thought it was neat that we were able to rent an apartment that had once been the boyhood home of Woodrow Wilson, our president from 1913–1921. Our female landlord was very accommodating and insisted we eat our meals with her family. I was impressed that she did no cooking on Sundays, but instead prepared Sunday's meal on Saturday.

I was awed by the massive buildings owned by the U.S. government and managed by the U.S. Department of Veterans Affairs. The facilities seemed like a mini city. John was on a locked ward, which I suspect meant he rarely left his confined quarters. He did not recognize Mama or me. For many nights after we returned home, I had terrible dreams of the intern with the massive ring of keys unlocking door after door on the many-storied building until finally John emerged.

My brother's future seemed fatal.

## A Nation Grieves

The death of Pres. Franklin Delano Roosevelt on April 12, 1945, 84 days into his fourth term of office, stunned Americans and shocked our international friends who trusted and leaned on him for guidance. He died of a cerebral hemorrhage at Warm Springs, Georgia, where the polio-stricken president often retreated from the White House to soak in the warm mineral spring waters at the retreat he had named The Little White House.

At the time of his death, FDR was the only president I'd ever known. I wept when I heard about his death over the radio and immediately began reading about it in a special edition of the *Waycross Journal Herald*. I felt like a member of my family had died. (The president was 63, and I was 14.) I remember cutting out the newspaper articles and making a scrapbook.

The train carrying FDR's body back to Washington, D.C. came through Waycross and eventually ended up at Hyde Park, New York. I recall watching the train as it passed by, not far from our house on Lincoln Street.

President Roosevelt consistently ranks as one of the top three best presidents the U.S. has ever had. Here is my list of his achievements that personally affected me:

- He calmed the nation's fears by leading Congress to create programs that gave Americans jobs and enacting banking safeguards to stabilize a shaky bank system.
- The 3,000,000 laborers who worked in the Civilian Conservation Corps (CCC) preserved many of the U.S. national parks.
- My income in my senior years has partially been dependent on the enactment of Social Security.
- The Tennessee Valley Authority (TVA) is an enormous asset to my adopted state of Tennessee by controlling floods and saving energy from generation to generation.

### A Reign of Terror Ends

Some 18 days after the death of FDR, Adolph Hitler, in his spacious 18-room underground bunker, swallowed a cyanide capsule and then shot himself in the head. Eva, his mistress of 22 years and his wife for one day, also swallowed a cyanide pill. She also poisoned her beloved Scottish terriers Negus and Stasi along with Hitler's German Shepherd Blondi. Someone hastily cremated the bodies of Hitler, Ava, and their dogs.

I recall a newspaper picture of that day showing a jubilant person celebrating, with a big iron ball attached to one of his ankles. Inscribed on the iron ball was the somber word "Japan!"

So vicious and diabolical were the war crimes of the Third Reich, I could never list all of them. Two were particularly heinous: the murder of Germans with mental or physical disabilities and the attempted extermination of the Jewish race.

Hitler and his henchmen decided that certain humans with disabilities or deformities, even if they were of German descent, were unworthy to live. They first targeted children from birth to age 3. Soon, the Nazis' murder of what they deemed marginal human beings grew to include anyone who Hitler considered "unworthy of life." This included people with epilepsy, alcoholism, birth defects, hearing loss, mental illness, personality disorders, vision loss, developmental delays, and certain orthopedic problems. Hitler's program began in 1939 and continued through the final days of the war. At least 70,000 people were murdered because they were deemed imperfect!

The number of Jews killed simply because Hitler and his cronies considered all Jews to be an inferior race and responsible for Germany losing WWI is mind-boggling.

According to the U.S. Holocaust Museum, Jews at that time numbered about 525,000 people in Germany, or 1 percent of the nation's population. In November of 1938 the Nazis burned more than 1,400 Jewish synagogues across Germany; vandalized Jewish homes, schools, and shops; murdered 91 Jews; and arrested 30,000 Jewish men and sent them to concentration camps.

Statistics from the Holocaust death camps from 1941–1945 are hard to ascertain since lots of the Nazi records were destroyed when, toward the latter stages of the war, they realized they were doomed to lose. The Third Reich maintained at least 25 main camps and more than 1,000 satellite camps. In the summer and fall of 1942 more than 300,000 Jews were deported from the Warsaw ghetto alone.

The most infamous concentration camp was Auschwitz, where more than 2,000,000 Jews were murdered. It is no wonder that many survivors described their imprisonment and torture at Auschwitz as hell on earth.

## The Buck Stops Here

Harry Truman had been FDR's vice president for only 82 days when FDR died. When Truman became president, international leaders were wary of his ability to forge agreement among our allies. But Truman proved he was a worthy successor to FDR and was our president when Germany surrendered, ending WWII in Europe.

After Germany's surrender Truman struggled with what to do about Japan's determination to continue fighting. Military advisors offered four options for forcing Japanese surrender: (1) Continue conventional bombing of Japanese cities; (2) Invade Japan; (3) Demonstrate the effectiveness of the atomic bomb on an unpopulated island; (4) Drop a bomb on an inhabited Japanese city.

Faced with the prospect of dropping an atomic bomb, Truman wrote, "It is an awful responsibility that has come to us." Contemplating his options as the war in the Pacific raged on, Truman met with other Allied leaders at the Potsdam Conference in the summer of 1945.

The Allies feared the Japanese would fight to the bitter end and force a full-scale invasion of the island itself, resulting in high casualties for both sides.

On July 26, 1945, the U.S. and its allies issued an ultimatum to Japan: surrender or face "prompt and utter destruction." But with no provisions being made in the Potsdam Declaration for the safety of its emperor, Japan refused the Potsdam terms.

Meanwhile, the U.S. government's secretive Manhattan Project, charged with creating an atomic bomb, reached a critical point. A nuclear detonation at a test site in Nevada had been a success. Now came the real test.

On August 6, 1945, three B-29 bombers departed from Tinian Field in the Mariana Islands in the Pacific Ocean for the explicit mission of dropping an atomic bomb on the Japanese city of Hiroshima, some 2,000 miles away.

Lt. Col. Paul Tibbets, the pilot in charge of delivering the death blow to Japan's stubborn resistance to surrender, had christened his B-29 Bomber *Enola Gay* in honor of his mother. Aboard the *Enola Gay* was "Little Boy," a huge nuclear bomb weighing 9,700 pounds.

In six hours all three B-29 bombers had reached Hiroshima, a logistics and supply military base essential to Japan's war effort. After a few mechanical adjustments the command to release Little Boy was given, and the bomb began spiraling down on Hiroshima.

The single atomic bomb dropped from the *Enola Gay* exploded over Hiroshima. Instantly, more than four square miles of the city became a massive heap of rubble and an estimated 90,000 people died.

That very day Mama and I had gone to hire a seamstress to do some mending jobs for us. When we got home our neighbor met us before we had time to go inside. She was very excited. "The U.S. has just dropped an atomic bomb on a Japanese city, and millions of people have died. Why don't you come over to our house and listen to the news?"

Mama hurriedly paid the taxi driver, and we joined our neighbors who were both happy and disturbed over the unfolding news. Our neighbor said, "It's terrible!! Millions of people are dead, including lots of women and children."

Truman had reluctantly chosen the drastic and enormously deadly step of obliterating Hiroshima and killing tens of thousands of civilians—not the millions our neighbors initially thought—in an effort to save as many American lives as possible by forcing the Japanese into surrender. When the bombing of Hiroshima failed to immediately induce Japan's surrender, three days later on August 9 the U.S. dropped a second, larger atomic bomb on the city of Nagasaki, killing an estimated 60,000–80,000 persons.

The following day Japanese emperor Hirohito signaled to the United States his desire to cease hostilities. He publicly announced Japan's surrender on August 15, with the formal paperwork signed on September 2.

The dropping of atomic bombs on Hiroshima and Nagasaki are credited with ending WWII, but also initiated a new phase of warfare known as "the Cold War."

### Lt. Col. Tibbets

Paul W. Tibbets in 1989 shared his reflections of Hiroshima with a reporter from the *National Museum of Nuclear Science and History*. I have selected some of his comments to help you understand the action from Tibbett's point of view.

"Since my early childhood I had been fascinated with airplanes. When I decided to drop out of medical school and join the Army my father was irate, but my mother said, 'Paul, if you want to fly, you go ahead. You will be all right.'

"During bombing raids over German towns, I refused to include morality issues into my bombing mission assignments. A medical doctor, while I was still in med school told me: 'Many med school students never make it to become doctors because they empathize too much with their patients.'"

Tibbets took his doctor friend's advice to heart. He reasoned that if he dwelt on the fact that his work resulted in the death of many innocent people, it would impede his military mission. Tibbets concluded, "My military mission was to drop the bomb, and that became the thing I was going to do to the best of my ability."

Tibbets also said, "In warfare there is no such thing as morality. It doesn't matter whether you are dropping atom bombs, or 100-pound bombs, or shooting a rifle. You have got to leave the moral issue out of it."

Tibbets learned of his assignment in the middle of September 1944, almost a year before he gave the command for Little Boy to be dropped on Hiroshima. During his preparation time everything Tibbets requested from the U.S. Pentagon was secretly granted to him under the code name Silverplate.

When asked about the specifics of dropping the massive bomb on Hiroshima, Tibbets replied, "My tail gunner exclaimed, 'Here it comes, meaning here come the shockwaves. When we looked, all we could see was a black boiling mess hanging over the city. The whole sky lit up when Little Boy exploded.'"

In his final thoughts Tibbets said, "I was clearly convinced in my own mind and had people telling me how much property and lives that the bomb would take when it exploded was nondiscriminatory. It took everything, and I have never lost a night's sleep over the deal. I am a bomber pilot whose job it is to destroy a target. I made up my mind that the morality of dropping that bomb was not my business. I was instructed to perform a military mission to drop the bomb. That was the thing I was going to do to the best of my ability. There is no such thing as as morality in warfare! I don't care if you're dropping  atom bombs, or 100-pound bombs, or shooting a rifle. You have got to leave the moral issue out of it."

### Can War Ever Be Justified?

Was the United States justified in going to war against Japan? Many historians and ethicists ascribe seven conditions to consider a war to be justified, including the following four:

1. *As a last resort*: Japan attacked the United States even while negotiations were going on in Washington between the two countries. After the U.S. declared war on Japan, both Germany and Italy declared war on the United States.

2. *Declared by a legitimate authority*: Both the U.S. President and Congress sanctioned the nation's war declarations in response to Japan's sneak attack on Pearl Harbor and Germany and Italy's declarations of war on our nation.

3. *Fight to right a wrong*: When another nation attacks your nation first, it is conceded that your country has every right to fight back.

4. *Have a shot at winning*: The Axis was made up of Germany, Italy, Japan, Hungary, Romania, and Bulgaria, with Germany, Japan, and Italy being the predominate nations. The United States and its Allies were Great Britain, Soviet Union, Australia, Brazil, Canada, Denmark, Greece, New Zealand, Netherlands, Poland, South Africa, Yugoslavia, China, and France. The Axis was outnumbered.

In 1945 when Japan finally surrendered, I immediately thought *Hooray, the war is over and we won*. Today I'm searching my mind and heart on the last three conditions that constitute a just war, and I find myself with ambivalent feelings and lots of unanswered moral questions. The following aspects of a just war cause me some angst:

*The goal is to restore the peace*: Ultimately, I feel the U.S. has emerged as a leader among the peacekeeping nations—that is, except for the Trump administration, which in my opinion greatly damaged our credibility as a peacekeeper on the international level.

When WWII ended, one of our Allies, the Soviet Union under Stalin, had a view vastly different from that of the U.S. and Great Britain. The Soviets became intent on spreading communism and wanted to extract harsh punishment on its aggressors. It seems to me that most of the Allies, including the U.S., were more generous after WWII to their aggressors than they were in WWI.

*Be only as violent as you have to be to right the wrong*: Violence, ruthless killings, and excessive bombings are commonplace in any modern war, and WWII was certainly no exception on the part of

the Axis of Evil or our Allied Forces. But I don't understand why
we had to drop not one but two atomic bombs to bring Japan to
surrender.

*Only kill the combatants*: When nations become embroiled in
a war, thousands of innocent civilians are killed deliberately and
unintentionally. Bomber pilots such as Paul W. Tibbets tell us that
good soldiers block out the moral issues on a bombing mission and
concentrates on doing the job to which they are tasked. Tibbets'
point of view of his job on Aug. 6, 1945 was to successfully drop
the bomb that had been predetermined by others and thus to end
World War II with the fewest possible American causalities. From
his viewpoint, his mission was highly successful.

However, more than 210,000 people died instantly from the
two atomic bombs dropped on Hiroshima and Nagasaki. It's fair
to assume that tens of thousands of those killed were babies, tod-
dlers, teenagers, mothers, grandparents, etc. The 210,000 does
not include those with glaring burns and myriad life-changing
conditions.

Tibbets may have been able to justify his decision to drop *Little
Boy* on Hiroshima by absolving himself completely from any accru-
ing moral issues. However, that is something I choose never to do.
My moral roots guide me daily in decisions, large or small. Most of
my moral judgments are in a state of becoming which means they
are often ideals that I, at some level, hope to attain.

I believe I have a moral responsibility to openly and aggressively
speak out against evil practices, while at the same time trying hard
to distinguish between the evildoers and the innocents.

I believe I have a moral responsibility to be loving, kind, and forgiving toward all people, with no preconditions required. The Bible
teaches me that I am my brother's keeper.

Some people would interpret my moral standards as naïve.
So be it! In Baptist churches when I worked with children in
Sunbeams and Girls in Action we often sang "Jesus Loves the Little
Children." The words are simple: "Jesus loves the little children, all
the children of the world. Red and yellow, black and white, they are
precious in his sight."

Does this make me a pacifist who believes there is no such thing as a just war? On an individual level that probably is my sentiment. Yet I firmly believe there are times nationally, as in WWII, when the only response a nation can take is to declare war on its oppressors.

American military leadership had tried three options, with limited success, to end the war with Japan. I was inclined to agree with President Truman's goal, which was to save American lives and to end the war. Since I don't recall having strong feelings concerning the dropping of two bombs on Japanese cities, I'm assuming as a teenager I lacked any moral feelings and simply expressed delight that the war would soon be over.

Today I find dropping atomic bombs on the unsuspecting cities of Hiroshima and Nagasaki to be inhumane. Acting like a beast just because your enemy fights on that level puts us on the same inhumane level as your enemy.

In war, and sometimes in decisions individuals and groups of people must make, I acknowledge that the right answers are not always easy to come by. Choosing the lesser of two evils doesn't leave me with a great deal of satisfaction, however.

---

*Central Baptist Church, like most, if not all, of the churches in Waycross, was packed with parishioners every Sunday during the war. It was hard to find anybody who wasn't affected firsthand by the war. My Aunt Maude, a Gold Star Mother, for more than a year displayed in one of her front windows a white, 12-inch flag with a red background. Centered on the white surface was one red star, telling everyone that her home had someone missing in action: It was William "Bill" Newman, her only son.*

---

# 1945–1946

### Move #19

Icouldn't believe it! A couple of months before I was due to finish the 9th grade at Waycross High, Mama unloaded on Kathryn and me a time bomb: At age 47 she had decided once again to get married.

I was at a vulnerable age, too young to be on my own, but old enough to have deep-seated feelings.

"Again?" I shouted, while shaking my head vociferously. "Have you forgotten Joe Millikin and how terrible that marriage was for all of us?"

Kathryn asserted her feelings by stomping her foot and saying, "I'm staying right here. If I have to, I'll take on a second job. Who is this guy you call Wallace, and how did you meet him?"

Mama was visibly upset by our reactions. She hastened to say, "Ila Ware told me about Wallace several months ago. He works as a night watchman with the Atlantic Coastline Railroad in Savannah. He owns his own home in a good neighborhood."

"Ila Ware," I said disgustedly. "If I remember correctly, she's the one who introduced you to Joe. I don't trust her match-matching skills!"

Kathryn and I failed in our attempts to dissuade Mama. True to her word, Kathryn remained on Lincoln Street. But in the summer of 1946, I moved with Mama to Savannah.

My first impression of my new stepfather was cynical. I wrote to my sister Darcile: "It's for certain Mama didn't marry him for his good looks. Wallace is tall, stout, bald-headed and has a bulbous nose."

Our new residence was #503 on Anderson Avenue, an unpaved street with paths instead of sidewalks. We lived in a one-story, white-frame structure with a hallway extending from the front door. Immediately to the right of the entrance was the living area that housed a fireplace. Through the arch to the right of the living room lay the dining room, which in turn opened to the kitchen.

To the left of the hallway entrance were two bedrooms, a bath, and a master bedroom. My bedroom was the first one, left of the living room. I had my own maple bedroom suit, something I'd never had before.

The furnishings were middle-class Americana, far better than ours on Lincoln Street but not super elegant. The house had two screened porches, one to the right of the living room and one that extended from the kitchen to the steps leading to the backyard.

## The Savannah of My Teens

August 26, 1946, like most summer days in Savannah, was steamy hot. Mama, Wallace, and I were standing on the corner of Anderson Avenue and Gwinnett Street, waiting to board a streetcar.

Wallace commented: "For as long as I can remember we've ridden streetcars to go places in Savannah. Soon we'll all be riding buses powered by gasoline. No longer will we ride on streetcars that travel on rails."

As we waited, perspiring profusely, we spent our time swatting at an army of invading mosquitoes. Finally, from a distance. we heard the clickety-clack of wheels turning on embedded rails. The tinkling bells alerted us that our streetcar was drawing nigh.

When we entered the corridor of the streetcar, the motorman was reversing the wooden seats. Perhaps our stop was located where the streetcar made its final stop before traveling forward again.

The city-run buses became my mode of transportation to Savannah High School. When the new school year began on the first Monday after Labor Day, I found myself daily at the same corner where we had waited to take a final ride on Savannah's last streetcar. And every day a swarm of mosquitoes bit me profusely! It wasn't four or five mosquitoes that came after me; it was more like 30 or 40!

I was always relieved when transit bus #10 arrived, with its destination reading East Savannah. After getting on the bus, I put my nickel in the token container and asked for a transfer slip. Bus #10 ended at the corner of Abercorn and Broughton in the heart of downtown Savannah. It was my main mode of transportation around the city, including mine and Mama's shopping trips.

During my teen years, a shopping mall didn't exist in Savannah. The closest thing we had to a mall was two competing department stores: Levy's and Adler's.

Levy's was a stone's throw of the bus stop at the corner of Abercorn and Broughton. Adler's was nearby on Broughton. The next four or five blocks of Broughton were lined with all sorts of specialty shops. There were several that sold only shoes.

Hats were a must-have item for most women, and Mama was no exception. Once Mama got Wallace off to work and me on my way to school, she spent many happy hours trying on hats in the host of millinery shops on Broughton Street. Mama had a thing for hats, and she was always looking for one that would make her appear taller. When she found a hat that she considered just right, you would have thought she'd found a pot of gold.

Those little 2x3-inch plastic cards we call credit cards were yet to be born in my teen years in Savannah. The famous phrase in those days was, "Put that on my account," or to simply say, "Charge it."

It wasn't long after we had moved to Savannah when Mama began spending too much on groceries. She was having a ball cooking for Wallace. I heard him tell her, "Honey, you're a great cook. However, you are feeding me so well, I can't wear any of my work pants."

## Morningside Baptist Church

One of the first things Mama and I did when we moved to Savannah was to look for a church home. Fortunately for us, a Baptist church was within five blocks of our house.

Morningside in 1946 was a newly organized Southern Baptist church and growing rapidly. Its members were friendly and made sure newcomers felt welcomed. On the first night we attended, a small crowd followed us to the stoop of the church's wood-frame entrance, encouraging us to come again. That was all it took. Mama and I both agreed that Morningside was going to be our church.

Throughout my teen years I listened to many sermons preached by my pastor, Rev. Cecil T. Underwood. Yet only one remains fixed in my memory forever.

One Sunday night he preached from Matt. 25:14-28 in which Jesus tells a story of a landlord who entrusted three of his servants with money to invest in his behalf. The amounts, or "talents," ranged from $1,000–$5,000 in our modern-day currency.

After a long absence the landlord returned and called on the three servants to hear what they had done with the money. The landlord was very pleased with the double investment returns of two of the servants. But the servant who had been given $1,000 hid the entire amount, supposedly for safekeeping. He hadn't even put it in a bank so it could draw a little interest! So, the landlord demanded that the hidden "talent" be given to one of the servants who had invested wisely.

In my teenage mind the word "talent" had a limited meaning. I equated it with people who through their oratory, singing, writing, artistic creations, or sheer charisma could sway masses of people.

When Pastor Underwood finished his sermon and while the invitation hymn was being sung, I confronted God with a special request. My prayer went something like this: "Lord, you know there isn't anything special about me. I can't carry a tune, my art attempts are pathetic, speaking in public is not my cup of tea, and I surely don't have gobs of money to give away. Pastor Underwood says you want us to use what we can do best. Lord, if I have a talent, you'll have to show me what it is because I'm convinced I haven't any."

Morningside had a large group of youth who attended Church Training, a program designed to help Christians become more mature in their faith journey. Our group was loud, irreverent, and decidedly more interested in upping their dating status than in developing our spiritual gifts.

The next Sunday I was minding my business and seated near the back of our youth assembly room when out of the blue our youth leader called on me to lead in prayer. I don't recall a word I uttered, but I do remember the praise my leaders heaped on me afterwards, with even a few of the youth making positive comments. I felt it was God's way of telling me, "You have a talent for bringing people together through voicing public prayers. Always use it wisely."

To our disheartened youth leader, who threatened almost every Sunday night to resign, I voiced a ray of hope. For me personally, our leader's response became a booster shot I sorely needed. For the first time in my Christian life, I felt I could contribute something valuable.

---

*Looking back today, I'm amazed by how patient and caring God is in helping us get of rid our useless spiritual baggage.*

---

### Puppy Love

Puppy love, the stage we go through in our teens when we think we'll die if a certain person doesn't return our love, may be one-sided or a mutual infatuation. It may be short-lived or can extend over an agonizing timeframe.

Mama attended Sunday School and Sunday morning worship services on a regular basis, but did not go on Sunday nights. I never wanted to miss going on Sunday nights to Church Training, so I had to navigate my way home alone. Walking home alone was fine during summer's extended hours of daylight. However, as summer's lingering splashes of light gave way to fall and winter's myriad shades of darkness, my friend John decided he needed to walk me home from church. (I suspect it was his father's insistence rather than John's personal choice.)

I was in seventh heaven since I secretly had a big-time crush on John. Week after week he walked me home, and never once did he grab my hand or begin uttering sweet nothings into my ears. I was bumfuzzled: *This isn't the way it's supposed to be. What's wrong with me?*

The months did an accordion squeeze, and the next time I saw John he had returned from spending a week at Ridgecrest, North Carolina, the ultimate vacation spot for Southern Baptists. He even came to my house to see me on a weekday. During his arts-and-craft sessions at Ridgecrest he had made me a wristband of twisted plastic raffia strips. It wasn't an engagement ring and probably cost less than five cents to construct, but the spin I put on the bracelet was that it magnified his love for me: *You'll see. Soon he's going to be telling our friends we're going steady.* This self-concocted affair of mine that I held on to for more than a year never materialized!

One day, by chance, I overheard John's sister say to a friend: "Lynelle is in love with John, but she doesn't know he's homosexual." All that time I had labored under the assumption that something was wrong with me. John became the second person in my life that I knew with same-sex preferences.

There were several boys along the way that claimed my interest, some with high-octane levels of testosterone, but the one I remember most was John. There is just something extra special about puppy love.

## Trouble in Camelot

Late one afternoon, Wallace's youngest son Thomas arrived unannounced and walked right into the bedroom where his daddy and my mama were lying. He began shouting angry, accusatory words at his daddy.

Thomas finally cooled his rhetoric and left. A few weeks later he came to have a meal with us, raising Mama's acceptability rating to a much higher level. Meanwhile, Thomas and I jawboned over passages of scripture—with both of us cocksure we had the last word from the Almighty.

I was in the middle of 10th grade at Savannah High, and Mama was having a hard time controlling her buying instincts. It seems she failed to understand that saying "Charge it" and "Put that on my account" could create a mountain of financial worries.

Wallace was exasperated and tried to reason with Mama. "Honey, you have to stop charging so many things at the grocery store. You've bought more at the grocery store in one week than I make in a month." Realizing he'd hurt Mama's feelings, he added, "My daughter Jeanie quit school and went to work when she was in the 10th grade. Maybe that's what Lynelle needs to do."

When Mama approached me with Wallace's idea of my quitting school and getting a job, I went ballistic. Using my pre-baptism vocabulary, I shouted, "I'll be dammed if I'm going to quit school. What does Wallace say to that?"

Mama sat in stunned silence for a long while. Meanwhile, I lost all control and continued ranting and raving. I yelled, "Send me to The Forks of the Hurricane! They'll take me in."

Mama was crying when she said, "I never dreamed you felt so strongly about going to school. Perhaps your Aunt Nevada will let you live with her until you graduate from high school."

"Mama, you don't understand! I can never become a missionary if I don't finish high school. Write to Aunt Nevada. The sooner I can leave this house, the happier I'll be."

For days it was like living in a war zone. Mama wrote to Aunt Nevada, Daddy's sister, asking if I could come live with her. While I waited for her answer, Mama tried to calm me down and reason with me, but I gave her the classic cold-shoulder treatment. When Aunt Nevada agreed to let me live with her, I began tossing my belongings in my well-worn suitcase.

Mama got in touch with Kathryn, telling her of my plans and asking her to meet me at the bus station in Waycross. Kathryn agreed to meet me and to see that I got to Aunt Nevada's house.

## Move #20

It was pitch-dark when we arrived at my aunt's house. Uldine, Aunt Nevada's daughter, clapped her hands and squealed, "Everybody, come see who has come to live with us! Now I'll have someone my age to talk with."

In addition to Uldine, Aunt Nevada had an older son, Charles Linwood, who was 18, and a son Lowell, who was younger than Uldine.

The first night when Uldine and I crawled into bed, we began hearing strident voices coming from her parents' bedroom. "Mom and Dad are always arguing," she said. "Mama wants Daddy to quit seeing his lady friend, and Daddy denies he's having an affair." She paused before adding," I don't know who to believe. I love Mama and Daddy and wish they could be happy together."

A mixture of happy, funny, holy, and sad events occurred to me during my stay at Aunt Nevada's, not far from my paternal grand-parents' home in The Forks of the Hurricane.

I was adamant in my choice of meats. One evening at the dinner table I exclaimed, "Steak is my favorite meat, but I can't stand the thought of eating goat meat."

The Lee family continued eating, making no response to my outburst. A few nights later as we sat down for dinner, Linwood said, "We have country fried steak tonight. Help yourself."

I took a generous serving and even asked for a second helping. Smacking my lips, I commented, "That steak is delicious."

The entire family burst into uncontrollable laughter. Linwood said, "Lynelle, that wasn't steak you ate. You just asked for a second helping of goat's meat."

## Brush Arbor Meetings

Not many people can boast of having a church in their front yard. However, In the spring of 1946 I was privy to an embryonic protracted meeting that became the seedbed for birthing Lee's Chapel Baptist Church near Alma.

My Uncle Keller and some men of the community built a brush arbor a short distance from the front of my aunt and uncle's house. The brush arbor was a rough shelter made by putting poles vertically in the ground and then adding additional poles laid across the vertical poles. When the poles were in place the men made a roof topping from the limbs of pine trees. Sniffing the distinct Christmas tree aroma emanating from the pine limbs sent my mind swirling to my childhood when the fragrance of pine trees and Christmas intertwined

My aunt and uncle hoped the brush arbor would usher in the beginning of a new church in their community. Soon a group of men, women, youth, and children began gathering under the brush arbor. Laughter, hugs, and kind words began spreading like a gentle breeze throughout the brush arbor. It wasn't long before we began singing the hymns of Zion.

When the preacher gave an altar call, Uncle Keller stepped forward, his eyes brimming with tears, and whispered something in the preacher's ear. Aunt Nevada also came forward and right there in broad daylight, before the entire crowd, they embraced in a mighty hug. I don't know what Uncle Keller told the preacher, but I do know the usual nightly arguments Uldine and I had grown accustomed to hearing ceased.

### Grandma's Parlor

Who would have thought it possible? Six years earlier I was an urchin with a penchant for dirt. Now I was living out a fantasy dream in Grandma's exclusive "holy of holies" parlor. How did this happen? Perhaps it was because Uldine's first name was Angie, short for Angelina, Grandma's name.

This I do know: Uldine and I spent many happy hours in Grandma's parlor. I read from the family Bible and with fervor preached to an audience of one. My message was always followed by a hymn of invitation. Due to my infamous lack of musical talent, Uldine's main contribution was giving me an occasional amen and playing hymns on the piano.

*Little did I know then how important this preaching episode, embedded deep within my psyche, would play out in my adult life. It certainly wasn't a usual diversion for 15-year-olds. The truth is, from the time I discovered I had a spiritual gift for reaching others through prayer, I likewise delighted in Bible study and expository teaching-preaching. This trait has increased throughout my adult years. Now I prefer to keep my mouth shut and spend my time encouraging those whose voices have been whitewashed or ignored by many Christians.*

### Inheritance Woes

The temperaments of my paternal grandparents, Alfred Colquitt Witherspoon Sweat and Angelina Davis Sweat, were vastly different. Grandma had opinions about both her friends and her foes and took pleasure in belittling others. She was a take-charge kind of person and an excellent cook who seemed happiest when she was reigning over a family reunion. Grandpa, who had strong political views, was prone to think before he spoke. He had an engaging smile and his eyes sparkled, making you think he could be a bit mischievous.

When I was 15 my mind was far removed from thoughts of inheriting a sum of money. However, that was not the case with

Grandma or Uncle Alfred Quarterman Sweat. (He was the one who thought that when his brother Ward died, his eight children should be sent to an orphans' home.) Behind the scenes, when they first realized Grandpa's health was failing, Grandma and Uncle Alfred convinced Grandpa to entrust Alfred Q. with the sole legal authority to execute Grandpa's will.

Grandpa Sweat

Grandpa Sweat had a severe stroke and wasn't expected to live. A huge crowd of relatives and friends began arriving at his house in The Forks of the Hurricane to say goodbye to Grandpa and to lend their support to Grandma and her sons and daughters.

In the lingering hours while Grandpa was still lucid, he indicated to a lady friend he wanted to see me. When I approached his bed, Grandpa began a stream of garbled words I couldn't understand. With tears in my eyes, I slowly left his side, wondering why Grandpa had asked to see me and what he was telling me.

Grandpa died on September 13, 1946, and a wake service was held in the parlor of the Sweat residence. All day and throughout the night a stream off people came to pay their respect to the patriarch of the Sweats and one of Pierce County's outstanding citizens and landowners.

By December of 1946, Alfred Q. began parceling out the property to Grandpa's heirs—but with one exception. The heirs of Ward Sweat were not mentioned. It was as if we didn't exist! My older brother Quentin was extremely upset over the omission of our daddy's family being excluded from the will, and was determined to change the situation.

---

*Hindsight is often helpful in unraveling knotty, unfair family problems. However, this inheritance issue still troubles me. The old Scottish proverb, "You can't make a silk purse out of a sow's ear," is as true today as it was thousands of years ago.*

*In my adult years I've often relived my bedside encounter with Grandpa. Maybe I'm grappling at straws, but I've convinced myself that Grandpa had recently become aware of plans to cut my family out of his will and he was attempting to tell me that wasn't what he wanted.*

*Legally my uncle had the authority to parcel out his daddy's will any way he chose. It is in the realm of morality that his decision reeks with injustice, however. One word describes the omission of Ward Sweat's heirs: greed.*

*I choose, in Christ, to reject being a slave to greed. For me it is liberating to focus on forgiving, giving, moving on, and leaving the judgment of others in the hands of my Creator.*

*Uncle Alfred Q. died in in 1953. From 1956 to his death in 1971 at age 52, Quentin devoted a relentless drive to rectify the inheritance situation. A few months prior to his death, he succeeded in a victory of sorts. Later, his son, Ward Sweat, issued each of Daddy's heirs $700.*

---

## Move #21

I was unhappy living at Aunt Nevada's, so sometime after Grandpa's death I received an invitation from my sister Darcile: "E.J. and I have jobs at the Naval Air Station in Jacksonville, and we're living in an apartment in a section of town called Ortega. I'm glad you chose to stay in school. I would like for you to come live with us until you finish the 10th grade. Mama is brokenhearted over your leaving. She misses you very much and wants you to come home."

My mind raced back to yesteryears at The Sycamores, our farmstead at Dixie Union, to a time when I was 5 years old and Darcile was 15. I giggled when I thought of her skating across our wooden front porch only to land on her butt in the yard. She'd had her hands full keeping me out of mischief. Like our brother John, she chose to finish high school.

During World War II, Darcile had taken up residence in every place her Navy husband E.J. was stationed. They had spent extended time in College Station, Texas, and in Baltimore, Maryland. On the weekends when E.J. was off duty, they would take many side trips. When the war ended and E.J. was discharged from the Navy, they had moved to Charleston, South Carolina, and often visited with E.J.'s parents.

Tears gently rolled down my cheeks when I read Darcile's letter. I thought to myself: *For the first time in their married life, they both have jobs and are living in their own apartment. She wants me to finish high school, and Mama misses me!*

I handed Darcile's letter to Aunt Nevada, who after reading it, agreed I should go live with my sister, who in many ways during my childhood had been a second mama to me. The following day Kathryn assisted getting me on a Greyhound bus in Waycross bound for Jacksonville.

Darcile met me at the bus station in downtown Jacksonville, and after giving me a big hug said, "You've grown so much since I last saw you that I almost didn't recognize you."

Blushing, I said, "Except for about 10 extra pounds and my hair needing to be cut, I'm about the same."

As I grappled with my scuffed-up suitcase—which looked as if it might burst open any minute—Darcile offered, "Let me help you with your suitcase."

But I grinned and said, "No, thanks. I just hope none of my unmentionables fall out on the street. I think my suitcase is ready to give up the ghost."

Upon boarding a transit bus marked Ortega, we rode and rode and rode. I turned to Darcile and asked, "How did you manage to move so far away from downtown?"

"Our apartment is close to the Naval Air Station where both E.J. and I work," she replied. "We're almost there."

In about five minutes Darcile reached up and yanked an overhead cord, letting the bus driver know we'd be getting off at the next stop.

After we crossed busy Roosevelt Boulevard, Darcile pointed to a church on her left and said, "That's our church. We go there every Wednesday night and two times on Sundays."

In less than 10 minutes we arrived at the apartment in a two-story, wood-frame house painted brown with yellow trimming.

"Sis," I asked, "Are you sure we're in Jacksonville? This neighborhood doesn't look like the Jacksonville I remember, and your house bears no resemblance to 705 Jackson Street!"

Darcile said, "Do you like the azaleas and black-eyed Susans growing in our yard?"

"Yes," I said. "They're beautiful and the huge live oak trees I saw in the park when we were on our way to your apartment make me lonesome for Savannah. I like the gigantic oaks spreading limbs and their gray tangles of Spanish moss."

### Robert E. Lee High School

I arrived at E.J. and Darcile's house on a Saturday. After church on Sunday, Darcile enlisted her friend Mary McClure to enroll me at Robert E. Lee High School.

As the registrar was typing my new schedule, my soon-to-be gym instructor appeared. The registrar introduced us. I could smell trouble before it started.

Muscular and vocal, the gym instructor announced: "You'll need a white gym suit with your name embroidered on the upper left pocket. Every Monday we have inspection. I expect you to appear in your starched and ironed gym suit and wearing your freshly cleaned white tennis shoes." Eyeing my flabby body, she added. "The penalty for not passing inspection is 15 laps around the gym." With her eyes flashing, she ended with "Have I made myself clear?"

"Yes, ma'am," I answered.

I could see right away that gym class was going to be a chore. The word "exercise" wasn't in my working vocabulary, and my klutzy body movements were an awkward giveaway. I was physically lazy and unmotivated.

I left after lunch on Saturday to go downtown to buy the items I needed for gym class. On my way back to Darcile's apartment I became fixated on getting off the bus at the right place, while unknown to me the bag containing my gym suit had slid into a crevice to the side of my bus seat. Recognizing my departure spot was next, I yanked on the overhead cord and grabbed the bag containing my tennis shoes, leaving my concealed gym suit behind.

Darcile was more than a little upset with me. "How could you? I'm not believing this!"

She called the transit dispatcher's office and told him what had happened. So, he traced the package and told us we could pick it up on the next scheduled run of the Ortega bus. Darcile and I were both waiting at the bus stop 30 minutes later when the friendly driver handed us my package. We thanked him and returned home. The embroidery work was yet to be done.

All is well that ends well. I arrived Monday morning with my freshly pressed gym suit and passed inspection. What a relief!

On another occasion I raced to get to English class in time to claim a back-row seat, hoping the teacher's view of me would be obscured. The emphasis for the day was on the writings of William Cullen Bryant. The hour was given to the closing portion of his poem, "Thanatopsis." We were instructed to analyze this passage:

> So live, that when thy summons comes to join
> The innumerable caravan, which moves
> To that mysterious realm, where each shall take
> His chamber in the silent halls of death,
> Thou go not, like the quarry-slave at night,
> Scourged to his dungeon, but, sustained and soothed
> By an unfaltering trust, approach thy grave,
> Like one who wraps the drapery of his couch
> About him, and lies down to pleasant dreams.

When the teacher asked the class what the poet was talking about, you could have heard a pin drop. I waited a minute or two and then spoke up: "The poet says we should live so we aren't afraid to die."

My teacher smiled broadly. "That's exactly right, Lynelle. I'm wondering, have you ever had anyone close to you die?"

I whispered, "My daddy died when a bolt of lightning hit where he was standing. My grandfather died in April of this year."

My classmates stared at me in disbelief. A few of the girls teared up.

In less than a week a middle-aged man with a large briefcase arrived during my English class and asked to speak with me. My teacher gave him her approval, so I went with him to a small room. He joked with me about getting a break from class and said he wanted to ask me some questions but not to worry if I didn't know the answer. He also said it was alright for me to guess at an answer. I don't know what that school psychologist found out about my mental acuity. Nothing in my school records made mention of it, so I'm assuming it didn't unearth any unusual results.

Meanwhile, back at my sister's apartment I began prowling around the premises. That's when I discovered three cartons of Hershey's chocolate delicacies placed high on a closet shelf. At first, I took one candy bar a day. Then my gluttony impulses kicked in and I literally gorged myself on chocolate bars!

After three months of living with my sister, we both decided it was time for me to go home. My last day of school at Lee High was current events day in my history class. When it came my turn, I shared an editorial cartoon. Its message escapes me, but my teacher's comment has lingered with me: "That's very good, Lynelle. I'm going to miss you and wish you could stay longer."

---

*My 15-year-old teenage ramblings fit into a classical profile. I daydreamed, forgot important details, refused to accept blame for my errors, overate, and was a master at procrastinating. At the same time, though often masqueraded, was a teenage girl hungry for adult approval, consumed by God-urgings that led her to believe God had special plans for her life. She was more determined than ever to finish high school. Perhaps unknown to her, God continued to increase her struggle to become more like him.*

---

### Move #22

I exited Lee High school on a Friday, and the following day I was waiting with my suitcase when Darcile got home from work. The two of us caught a transit bus to the Greyhound bus terminal and bought two tickets for Savannah, the place where I had left angry and disturbed. I wished I could erase the harsh ugly words I'd said to Mama prior to my leaving home to live with Aunt Nevada. Unfortunately, I couldn't.

I'd assumed Mama had agreed with my stepfather, Wallace, about my quitting school. According to Darcile, that wasn't true. Mama had written to her, saying I'd been so upset over the thought of quitting school that I refused to give her a chance to tell me how she felt about the idea.

As we traveled toward Savannah, I did some deep soul-searching: Darcile and Mama were right. The closer we came to our destination, the higher rose my level of anxiety.

Shades of night were creeping over the city of Savannah when our bus arrived at 7 p.m. at the Greyhound terminal. I spotted Mama standing on the unloading platform. A minute later she grabbed me in her arms and said, "Glory be! My baby has come home!"

Before the night ended, Mama and Wallace and I had mended our differences and Darcile planned to return to Jacksonville early on Sunday morning.

Thus ended my six months of wanderings.

# 1946–1948

### Back Where I Belong

It was so good to be back home in Savannah! My folks and I talked until close to midnight. Then I snuggled up in my bed and was still sound asleep at noon the following day when Mama came to my room and gently shook me.

"Get up. Dinner is almost ready, and Darcile will soon be leaving to go home."

I dragged myself out of bed, crawled into my jeans, and followed my nose to the dining room table laden with my favorites: roast beef, potato salad, green beans, corn on the cob, vine-ripe tomatoes, and yeast rolls. For dessert we had banana pudding, the likes of which had long been one of Mama's specialty dishes.

On the Wednesday following my return to Savannah, I talked with the Sunday School superintendent at Morningside Baptist Church about becoming a teacher with the 4- and 5-year-olds. The powers that be felt I needed to remain in the youth department, but offered me an alternative ministry option.

Morningside had recently accepted a small rural church some 15 miles from Savanah as a mission project. The outreach committee offered me the job of teaching Sunday School at the mission every Sunday afternoon to a mixed group of attendees. I accepted the task with gusto.

For several months I went with two deacons from our church every Sunday to a one-room, wood-frame church recessed in a wooded, seemingly forgotten area. When we turned off the highway we traveled for several miles over unpaved roads, more commonly known as pothole trails. If I hadn't known better, I would have sworn we were in Appalachia. The spokeswoman for our group was someone I'll call "Mrs. Fix-It."

Mrs. Fix-It's face was a patchwork of rutted wrinkles bearing weather-beaten reminders of unrelenting exposure to the sun. Clad in a homespun tattered dress, overlaid with an apron, her feet were covered with heavy-duty oxfords. Her son, or perhaps he was her grandson, was always present. He came wearing a clean pair of overalls, too short for his growing body, and his hair was slicked down with a little dab of Brylcreem. I don't think his feet had ever seen a pair of shoes.

I never taught a lesson. Instead, I preached. All 10 or 12 attendees took to me like bees swarming around a honeysuckle vine.

Mrs. Fix-It considered herself a matchmaker. I became skittish when after several months she announced her child wanted to marry me. What a mess! I shook my head in disbelief. There was no way I could imagine being married to a grade school dropout from a family living on the cusp of poverty in a dwelling located in a desolate part of Chatham County.

At some point we moved from gathering outside in a semicircle to inside the 8'x12' church building. I became quite comfortable expounding on the scriptures from the pulpit stand, with no one ever raising any objection.

The ladies began tidying up the inside of the church edifice. They swept, dusted the wooden pews, and brought cut flowers for the pulpit.

After several months an associational youth gathering held at Morningside captured my interest, and I never returned to our mission church.

## Part Child, Part Adult

Mrs. Allen, the leader of our mission group at Morningside Baptist called Girls' Auxiliary (G.A.s), was a mixture of piety and ineptness. While no one would question her faith, Mrs. Allen was sadly lacking when it came to understanding and motivating teenagers.

Our group of six girls talked Mrs. Allen into taking us to Savannah Beach, some 20 miles away, for an overnight retreat. She agreed to take us if we would read our mission study book while we were there. She told us our curfew time to be back in our room was 8:00 p.m.

After agreeing to the curfew, two of the girls in our group—twins—decided they wanted to roller-skate. However, the skating rink located on Savannah's beach pavilion opened at 7:30, as darkness began edging over the horizon, and stayed open until the bewitching toll of midnight.

On Saturday evening the twins convinced the rest of us to break our curfew so we could watch them show off their roller-skating expertise. We huddled together and made plans to eat dinner with our leader, while at the same time making sure she saw us clutching our mission study books. After our meal we each exited, pretending to go to our room. Instead, we tip-toed down the outside stairs and raced for the pavilion.

About 8 o'clock, assuming we were all snuggled up on our cots and reading our assigned book, Mrs. Allen proceeded to lock the entrance screen door.

At the skating rink, when the wall-mounted clock pointed to 10:00 p.m., I began feeling guilt pangs and convinced my G.A. friends we should return to our apartment. They agreed. When we got back to the apartment, we were in for a big surprise: The door was locked!

We discussed our options: "Do we rouse Mrs. Allen out of bed, confess what we have done, and ask for her forgiveness?"

Instead, we did something only a group of teenagers would ever devise: We decided to sleep on the upstairs porch chairs. We batted away the hours giggling, sharing ghostly tales, and doing everything but sleeping. Each of us was a sight for sore eyes when Sunday's light began trickling over our hideaway.

I don't recall any of us telling Mrs. Allen what we had done, but I do remember that we all showed up that same morning for church on Tybee Island. We occupied the back row of the center aisle and kept pinching each other to stay awake. After church we returned to our apartment, ate lunch, packed up, and drove back to Savannah.

## Immanuel Baptist Church

During my teenage, years Southern Baptists excelled in associational work that helped individual churches to find out what programs, etc. other churches were having. During an associational

Church Training youth gathering, Immanuel Baptist Church—off busy Waters Avenue—oversaw the program that met at Morningside Baptist. I struck up a conversation with their leader after the meeting ended, and she invited me to speak to their youth group. I accepted and thus began my brief exodus from Morningside to Immanuel.

In 1948, while a member of Immanuel, I entered my first Speakers Tournament. I chose the topic, "Seeing the World Through the Eyes of Christ," and came in second among several contestants vying for the honor at the associational level. Immanuel honored my entry by paying for me to attend YWA (Young Women's Association) Week at Ridgecrest, North Carolina.

### Unforgettable Ridgecrest

From the moment I left Savannah on a Greyhound bus for Ridgecrest, North Carolina, I was on an emotional high. To begin with, my traveling experiences had been limited to Waycross, Jacksonville, and Savannah. By the time we arrived in Chattanooga, I began hopping from one side of the bus to the other. Huge boulders of stone covered with trees claimed my attention.

Much to the amusement of the other passengers I yelled, "I can't believe this! Did you all see those mountains?"

One of the men said, "You're looking at Lookout and Signal Mountains. Where are you from?"

"I grew up in Waycross, Georgia, where the land is flatter than a flapjack just off the griddle."

"That figures," the man said. "Where are you going?"

"I'm on my way to Ridgecrest," I answered.

The man then told me, "As we get closer to North Carolina, you're going to see lots more mountains. I hope you enjoy your visit."

Late that afternoon after registering and receiving a fistful of information, I was escorted by a handsome young volunteer to my cottage apartment.

It didn't take me long to discover the Nibble Nook, whose servings of double-dipped cones of mouthwatering ice cream were legendary. At noon I ambled over toward the dining hall and found myself surrounded by friendly young Texans who, seeing I was alone, invited me to sit at their table. It wasn't long before the Texas delegation raised the rafters with their rendition of "The Eyes of Texas Are Upon You."

Four of our speakers, Theron Rankin, Virginia Wingo, Sue Saito, and Chester Swor made indelible marks on my life.

### Theron Rankin

We sat in awe, with tears streaming down our faces as Theron Rankin, surrounded by a cadre of missionary associates, told of his internment experiences.

He had been in Hong Kong in December 1941 when the Japanese attacked Pearl Harbor. As a foreigner he was not allowed to leave, so he quickly gathered the several Baptist missionaries in the region into an apartment building over the harbor. They hid there for 17 days while enduring constant bombings. Eventually, the whole city had to surrender, and the Americans were marched as prisoners to Stanley Internment Camp.

The prisoners were not beaten or tortured, but they were slowly starving to death. The rice contained as many weevils as it did rice, but that was all they had to eat. At times they went days without eating and learned to share food with the children and others in camp with them. Even in prison, Rankin was a leader, overseeing food and relations among the whole camp. The prisoners were released in 1942 and Rankin returned to America, a shell of a man. But before long he was out preaching and raising support for mission causes

### Sue Siato

Dressed in a stunning kimono and with an effervescent smile, Sue Siato spoke about her mission work in Hawaii. At Ridgecrest she shared with us about the religious customs of her Japanese ancestors. Japanese by birth and now a citizen of Hawaii, Sue became my first contact with someone whose racial background was different than mine. Through my association with Sue, my world became much bigger.

## Virginia Wingo

One morning while at Ridgecrest, I isolated myself on a vacant mountain peak to pray. Soon a lanky woman, probably in her late 30s or early 40s, asked if she could join me. I nodded my agreement.

"I'm Virginia Wingo, missionary to Rome, Italy," she said. "Please tell me about yourself."

I told her my name and where I was from and then asked, "Ms. Wingo, how did you know God wanted you to serve as a missionary in Italy?" She answered:

> I grew up in Louisiana with my dad, mother and older brother. I made my profession of faith when I was 7 and was baptized by my father, who was also the pastor of our church. My brother and I started a club we called Young Disciples to help people. We met once a week, after school, at our church. We invited others to join our group. Daddy often had missionaries speak at our church, and I also heard and met missionaries from faraway places. I began thinking I might be a missionary one day. After graduating from college, I began teaching school. I enjoyed being a teacher but could not squelch a gnawing feeling that God had other plans for me. While I was a student at Carver School of Missions in Louisville, Kentucky, during my prayer times God opened certain opportunities for me while blocking others. Lynelle, are you thinking God may want you to become a missionary?

"Yes, ma'am. I think about it night and day, but I don't have the money to go to college. Do you suppose that's God's way of telling me I'm not to be a missionary?"

Virginia Wingo clasped my hand in hers and said, "If God wants you to attend college, he'll open a door that will enable you to go. Keep praying and stay willing to serve wherever he needs you most. It's been wonderful talking with you, Lynelle. I think it's about time we get some breakfast."

My mountain-top talk with Virginia Wingo became my first time ever to talk with someone currently serving as a missionary. She left a lasting impression on my future hopes.

## Chester Swor

Chester Swor's drawing power, especially with young people, was enormous. Thousands of us packed the auditorium at Ridgecrest, waiting to hear him.

An English professor at Mississippi College, he was no stranger to overcoming obstacles. Stricken with polio when it was time for him to enter the first grade, he spent the next six years struggling to stay alive. When Chester was 12 years old the disease was cured, but he was left permanently lame with one leg three inches shorter than the other. As a youngster, he began wearing a heavy brace over both of his legs.

As he hobbled toward the microphone station at Ridgecrest, the crowd burst into a thunderous applause. Doctor Swor looked as if a strong puff of wind would sweep him away. Quite to the contrary, his words found lodging in my heart. He talked about us always keeping a jar of honey nearby, to sweeten the sorrow either we or a friend might be experiencing. He spoke about spreading honey lavishly on our parents and friends.

## Some Problems Never End

I hadn't been back home 15 minutes from my trip to Ridgecrest before Mama exclaimed, "You've changed! Your face is glowing."

"Thank you, Mama," I said, giving her a super hug. "You've spent your entire life loving and taking care of me. I hope you like the new me."

But waiting in the anteroom of my life was a heavy-handed decision.

Mama had received a call from the administrator at the VA hospital in August, where John had been on a locked ward for many years. He said, "Mrs. Wallace, we need you to come talk with us about your son. Some of our doctors know of an operation that could make a great difference in his life. When can you come to Augusta?"

Mama didn't hesitate. "I can come on Wednesday."

"Good," responded the director. "We'll look forward to seeing you on Wednesday."

Mama arrived at the VA hospital on Wednesday as she had promised. Once the official protocol was completed, John's case was turned over to a new doctor. The first thing he did was to have someone bring John in so Mama could have a firsthand view of how rapidly his condition was deteriorating.

All of Mama's attempts to converse with John were futile. There was no spark of memory, simply a vacant, lifeless stare. Mama shook her head sadly, biting her lower lip as the guards in charge returned John to his locked ward.

The lead doctor said, "Mrs. Wallace, lately we have had lots of success with a certain type of operation on patients with severe mental problems and are interested in seeing if we can help patients like John."

Mama began wringing her hands. "What are the risks involved?"

The doctor's face turned red, revealing he was anxious to have this matter resolved, sooner rather than later. "Mrs. Wallace, I'm sure you know that with John, it's for sure if he lingers here on a locked ward much longer, he's going to die. While there are always risk factors when you do anything to someone's brain, it's also possible John may regain his mental acuity and be able to go home with you. The choice is yours. Go home and talk with your family about what we have discussed, and then call me as soon as you reach a decision."

Mama thanked the doctor and returned home. She told me about her conversation with the doctor and began making calls to Darcile, Quentin, and Kathryn. We were all in agreement that John's chances were better by having a lobotomy than doing nothing, so Mama called the VA to set up a date and place for the procedure to be done.

The surgery was scheduled for St. Vincent's Hospital in Jacksonville. I remember how Mama, Darcile, Kathryn, and I walked the floor in the waiting room as we waited for John to come out of the recovery room. The operation was speedy, and we were soon allowed to see John, his head bandaged. The doctor kept our encounter short and insisted we leave John's room but stay close by.

*In the 1940s, after WWII, veterans' hospitals were overflowing with mental patients. Linwood Hospital in Augusta, where John lingered in a comatose condition, was no exception. So huge was the number of patients that physicians were prone to try anything to alleviate the problem.*

*According to an article appearing in* Wired *on Nov. 12, 2008, the United States performed more pre-frontal lobotomies than any other country. The exact number isn't known, but from the 1940s to the 1960s, the estimate is 40,000–50,000. The two most prominent people in the United States performing lobotomies were Walter Freeman and James Watts.*

*The procedure called for inserting an icepick-like instrument above the patient's eyeball and just above the tear duct. Then the doctor would hammer the icepick into the patient's skull and wiggle the tip of the pick around. The operation took about 10 minutes, with the results ranging from fair to disastrous!*

When John awoke from surgery, he seemed alert and called each of us by name. We were elated! For us, a miracle had occurred. A problem arose shortly thereafter, however, and we were warned that he may have to use a catheter for the rest of his life.

*According to Dialysis Patient Citizens Educator Center, catheters are necessary when someone cannot empty their bladder. If the bladder isn't emptied, urine can build up and lead to pressure on the kidneys. The pressure can lead to kidney failure, which can be dangerous.*

Fortunately, John's kidney functions returned to normal, and within two weeks John returned to our house on Anderson Avenue.

He decided he wanted to raise rabbits, so Mama hired someone to build four wire cages in the backyard, and she bought huge bags of bunny food, etc. This project was short-lived, however—probably because the rabbits kept multiplying! John's interest next turned to art. Using acrylic paints, he produced exquisite pictures of roses. That venture was also short-lived.

John had been living with us for several months when he decided he wanted his own place. Mama found him an apartment downtown, not far from Savannah's historic Pink House, but that arrangement didn't work. Soon his neighbors were complaining about queer visitors, and John was evicted.

---

*In 1948, gays and lesbians had no legal rights. Georgia considered homosexual behavior as sodomy. Lambda's legal web site states that Georgia's sodomy law declared any consenting adult who practiced oral or anal sex, gay and non-gay, in Georgia to be guilty of committing a felony, punishable by 20 years in prison. It was not until 1998 that Georgia's Supreme Court struck down its sodomy law.*

---

Mama began grasping for answers until she remembered that the entire downstairs part of her house in Waycross was currently vacant. Maybe, just maybe, John could make a go of it there. She accompanied him to Waycross, helped furnish his apartment, and gave him money to buy groceries and other necessities. No sooner than Mama left, however, John's desire for homosexual activity kicked in. A few months later, Mama had no choice but to send him back to the VA hospital in Augusta. This time he was assigned to an open ward.

## My Senior Year

When I moved to Savannah in 1946, I attended Savannah High. But when I returned to Savannah in 1948 from living in Alma and Jacksonville, I enrolled at Commercial High School, housed at 35th and Bull streets. We either brought our lunches from home or ate at a nearby drugstore that had a lunch counter. I often ate at the drugstore with my friend Betty Jarrell, a friend I had met at Morningside Baptist Church during Baptist Training Union.

Many veterans, taking advantage of the benefits of the G.I. Bill of Rights, were among my classmates. The Servicemen's Readjustment Act of 1944 provided a range of benefits for returning WWII veterans, such as low-interest loans to purchase a home or start a business or a farm, and one year of unemployment compensation.

In addition, dedicated payments of tuition and living expenses provided veterans the opportunity to attend high school, college, or vocational school. This bill, more commonly called the G.I. Bill, was highly successful for most veterans. However, it discriminated against African Americans, especially in the South.

My senior year at Commercial High was full of challenges. In addition to dealing with the family dynamics involving John, the reality of my chances of ever having enough money for college were fast evaporating. I had pretty much acclimated myself to someday becoming a church secretary.

Typing class seemed overwhelming. All the letters and numbers on my typewriter were blank, but a huge reproduction of our keyboard was mounted on the wall where we could see it. It seemed like forever before I ever typed anything except *a-s-d-f* with my left hand and *:-l-k-j* with my right hand. Gradually we added the g and h keys to our repertoire.

I continued to excel in my American history class, but English grammar class was an entirely different matter. Moods, clauses, tenses, punctuation, you name it ... they gave me trouble!

On the night before graduation day, we had a dance and banquet at the DeSoto Hotel. I had the honor of offering the prayer before we ate. I recall my typing teacher, who was Jewish, telling me to omit the phrase, "in Jesus' name," which I did.

I don't recall how I got from home to the De Soto Hotel, but for sure I wasn't escorted to the hotel by my date. I blew my chance of that happening more than a month before the event took place. I'd made a disastrous phone call, asking a boyfriend of mine to take me out on a Saturday night.

He told me, "Saturday is my hardest workday at the grocery store. That's when we restock items. I seldom go out on Saturday nights. I usually go home, eat supper, take a bath, and go to bed."

I'd long since made up my mind that all boys were interested in was sex. That's when I uttered words that I had no intention of fulfilling. "Well, if you change your mind, I promise to make it worth your time."

My friend, assuming I had just consented to have sex with him, said, "In that case I'll pick you up at 7 o'clock."

We soon hung up, and I was left with two days and nights to fret over my stupid remark.

We had no sooner parked at Savannah's teenage, food-loving drive-in when my friend reached in his pocket as he prepared for his reward. I was flabbergasted and immediately began making excuses.

We didn't have sex, but I did inherit an angry and unforgiving boyfriend. We never had another date!

Later, on prom day, from a postage-size corner of the De Soto hotel lobby, a three-piece band welcomed me upon my arrival.

Have you ever tried convincing someone to hang-glide who faints at the thought of heights? There I was, standing in my borrowed evening gown, trying desperately to keep my over-inflated boobs halfway covered. I had never danced! I had no earthly idea what I was supposed to do. My body stiffened, and my two feet seemed loaded with lead.

Our class counselor nudged an innocent-looking classmate to give me a twirl. The guy dutifully obeyed. Twice around the small dance area, and he returned me to my bystander's post. You can bet I didn't linger long with the dancers, but hastened to find my way to the banquet hall.

## Move #23

After graduating from high school, I was like a fish trying to swim on dry land. Virginia Wingo, the missionary to Italy, had assured me that if God wanted me to go to college, he would provide a way. My task, according to her, was to follow every door God opened and to be willing to serve anywhere he needed me.

In early May my sister Darcile telephoned me. "Lynelle," she said, "My baby is due May 21. Can you come to Jacksonville and help me?"

"Mama and I were talking about you and your baby-to-be last night. She suggested I should come and lend you a hand. I'll pack my suitcase right away and leave for Jacksonville tomorrow morning. Don't worry about having someone meet me at the bus terminal. I'll catch a taxi to your new address on Manitou Avenue"

We ended our conversation and, after telling Mama of my plans, I began piling my clothes into my old suitcase.

I arrived on schedule at Darcile's house, but almost went into shock when the cab driver said, "Miss, that will be $15." I was thinking he'd charge me $5 or at the most $10.

Darcile, looking as if she'd swallowed five big watermelons, greeted me warmly and then showed me where I'd be sleeping. In a little while she took me on a tour of her new house. I couldn't believe the matchbox size of her kitchen.

Sensing my surprise, Darcile said, "We hope someday to enlarge the kitchen."

## The Answer Comes

While staying with Darcile, I attended the church where she and her husband were active members. Ortega Baptist Church was having expansion woes. The only place where our youth could meet was in the kitchen of the church's recently erected pastorium. It was in that kitchen during Sunday School that God's answer met me face to face! Our teacher, who was also our pastor's wife, was Leona Althoff.

I don't recall the particulars that led up to my revealing how badly I wanted to become a missionary, but I explained that to become a missionary I'd have to go to college for four years. I finished by adding, "With no money for college, I'll have to give up my missionary dream."

Mrs. Althoff asked, "Lynelle, do you really want to go to college? Are you willing to go far away? Are you willing to work to pay for your college tuition?"

"Yes," I answered. "Do you really think such a place exists?"

Mrs. Althoff smiled and said: "When I was your age, I also wanted to go to college but had no money. A Baptist school for girls in Texas, Baylor College for Women, gave me a six-hour-a-day work scholarship. That's how I got my college degree. Would you like for me to write Baylor and ask them to accept you as a candidate?"

I didn't wait a split second! I instinctively knew God was speaking through my teacher to give me my long-sought answer. "Yes, I'll go to Texas. Yes, I'm willing to work to pay for my tuition. And yes, please write to the school for me!"

A week later I got a letter from Mary Hardin-Baylor College saying the college would be happy to have me as a member of the class of 1953. Because my daddy had been a minister, they awarded me a scholarship of $100. The school also gave me a work scholarship that allowed me to pay for my tuition through work I would do in the dining area, such as setting the tables prior to eating times, waiting on the tables during mealtime, and scraping dirty plates and sending them through the mammoth dishwasher.

## Texas Bound

Clutching my college acceptance letter in my hand, I rushed back to Savannah and shared my good news with Mama and with Pastor Gaddis at Immanuel Baptist Church. Immanuel gave me a scholarship fund of $100, and my two sisters also contributed to my tuition fund. Mama, using her "charge it" status, spared no expense in replenishing my wardrobe. With all this assistance, I would need to work only four hours a day in the college dining area.

I left Savannah on a one-way ticket to Belton, Texas, aboard a Greyhound bus and with $25 in my pocketbook. After riding for more than 12 hours, we finally arrived at Belton's tiny bus depot. With my suitcase in tow, I plopped down in a nearby seat, waiting to be escorted to the campus. Without warning, a small army of gigantic bugs began encircling me with aerial leaps. These critters made our Savannah mosquitoes look inferior.

Momentarily, I wavered. *What have I gotten myself in to? I'm more than a thousand miles from home, have only $25 to my name, don't know how to deal with these hopping critters, and no one has arrived to take me to the college.* That thought was washed away, though, when a young man arrived to escort me and my baggage to my room in Ely Pepper dormitory.

Before I could open my suitcase, I was met by a Texas girl, whose big smile and welcoming words warmed the cockles of my heart. She said, "Hurry, girl, find your stockings. It's time for supper."

I scrambled through my suitcase, tossing my belongings hither and yon as I tried to find my stockings.

Finally, Pat said, "Stop looking for your stockings. Since you just got here, I'm sure it will be okay for you not to wear stockings tonight. After we eat dinner at Hardy Hall, I'll take you to our campus sing-along."

It had been an exceedingly long day. But instead of feeling exhausted, I felt exhilarated. To be sure, tomorrow would bring its challenges. But tonight, I felt acceptance, friendship, and love. I sensed that God and I would be ready for all the tomorrows that lay ahead.

# CLOSING THOUGHTS

How do you thank someone, now deceased, who forever altered your life? There are several people to whom I owe belated thank-you's: my mama, Cleo Jordan Sweat; my brother John; Leona Lavender Althoff; and, most importantly, Jesus.

**Thank you, Jesus, for Mama.**

She went through the pangs of birthing me on Feb. 24, 1931, four months before her beloved husband was killed by a bolt of lightning.

When creditors foreclosed on her house in Waycross, with tear-stained eyes, she moved herself and her eight children to her farm property, far removed from her supporting sisters.

During the most formative years of my life, she was there for me 24 hours a day. The youngest of 10 children and accustomed to a carefree childhood, she adapted with finesse to living on a shoe-string existence.

When her finances hit rock-bottom, seven years after Daddy's death, she married a smooth-talking ne'er-do-well, who conned her into taking out a loan on her farm. Then he left for Jacksonville, leaving his three youngest children in her care. She was determined to salvage her marriage, despite the protest of her children against their fabricated stepfather. Only after he admitted to being unfaithful to their marriage vows did she entertain thoughts of divorcing him, selling her farm, and buying a house in Waycross. There she renewed her spiritual vows that had gone AWOL while she was married to Joe.

Called upon to care for her gay son, whose sexual identity she was ill-equipped to embrace, she felt forced to have him committed to the veterans' hospital in Augusta, and ultimately agreed for him to have a lobotomy.

Her love, courage, stories, and laughter are among my most treasured inheritances.

## Thank you, Jesus, for John.

He was the pied piper who invaded our bleak existence at The Sycamores as a grotesque scarecrow telling spine-chilling stories. He bolstered my ego with a special outfit for my entry into kindergarten. At Haywood he averted a disaster by snuffing out my lighted Roman candle.

When money was scarcer than a hen's tooth, I can't remember a time when gifts didn't arrive from him. He knew how to make a child feel loved and very special.

His gift of a subscription to the *Atlanta Journal* exposed my mind to conflicting political and social viewpoints. He seemed to know how isolated my rural community could be.

With honesty and courage, in a time when having a same-sex attraction was legally called sodomy, he shared his sexual identity with his family.

His love for the arts, especially books, theater, and dance remain among my richest treasures. The inscription on his tombstone sums up the loving esteem my family had for him. It reads, "He was the sunshine of our home."

## Thank you, Leona Lavender Althoff.

While I was working on my memoir *Tarnished Haloes, Open Hearts*, I began searching for information on Leona Lavender Althoff. My research efforts were futile!

In 2010 I attended my 50th college reunion at the University of Mary Hardin-Baylor and talked with fellow alumni Betty Sue Beebe who was then serving as the administrator of the university's recently established archives building. She told me her efforts to find anything about Leona Lavender, like mine, had produced no results. Any records the college had on Leona were burned in the devastating fire of the 1950s that destroyed the administration building. It was if Leona Lavender never existed!

In 2020, when I began putting together my thoughts on the people who had a great impact upon my life, my thoughts immediately turned to Leona Althoff, the woman who had offered me an inheritance I couldn't refuse. This led me to redouble my ancestry quest. This time my search, while still incomplete, was more fruitful. What follows is what I know for sure about Leona L. Althoff:

- Leona was born in February of 1898 in East Bernard, Texas. The 1900 U.S. census lists her as Leonora Lawandawski, age 2, in Wharton, Texas. Her father (34) was John Lawandawski, and her mother Ella Lawandawski. Both parents were born in Texas. Leona had two older sisters, Elmer and Tenie, and someone named Tom is listed as Boarder.

- Newspapers in Nashville, Tennessee published articles that indicate Lena was actively involved as a worker at the Baptist Sunday School Board from 1928–1936. A picture of her was posted in the *Nashville Banner* on Dec. 9, 1936, along with her wedding announcement to Dr. Charles Benjamin Althoff. They were married on Dec. 20, 1936, in Nashville. The announcement in *The Freeport (TX) Facts* revealed that she had worked for the Baptist Sunday School Board in Nashville since 1925.

- Records obtained from the Florida Baptist Historical Society indicate Charles and Leona had one daughter, Marilyn Gay, born on Feb. 4, 1939.

- According to ancestry.com, Charles and Leona took two trips to Southampton, England, the birthplace of Charles Althoff: In September of 1937, when Leona was 39, they took what was possibly a delayed honeymoon. In June of 1956, when Leona was 58, they traveled to Southampton again.

- Charles Benjamin Althoff died at age 91 on May 5, 1970, in Tallahassee, Florida, and is buried in Roselawn Cemetery there.

- According to *U.S. Social Security Applications and Claims, 1936–2007*, Leona A. Lavendusky married Mayes Behrman in Leon County, Florida on June 5, 1977.

- Leona died on Dec. 14, 1987 at age 89, and is buried next to Charles Althoff in Roselawn Cemetery in Tallahassee.

Although my research about Leona gave me lots of answers, I still had questions. I wondered where she lived between 1898 and 1925. I wish I knew if Leona went directly from high school to college. If she did, she would have perhaps been affected by WWI. I wish I knew her college major. Perhaps it was journalism or library science. I wish I knew if she was employed elsewhere before accepting a job at the Baptist Sunday School Board.

Sometimes the things we inherit are so visible that they make our hearts tremble with expectancy. Some people may see the unfolding events that happened to me during a Sunday School youth session in the late 1940s as a happenstance. I beg to differ. I see it as a time when God provided me with an answer to my prayers. It was not pure chance that God used Leona Althoff to change forever the direction of my life. As someone who worked six hours every day to pay for her college tuition, she spoke to me from experience. Sensing my willingness to do likewise, she wrote a letter of recommendation in my behalf to Mary Hardin-Baylor College. God used Leona to open for me a door of opportunity that led to the inheritance of an education that remains exceedingly valuable.

### Thank you, Jesus.

For some unknown reason to me you chose, perhaps from my mother's womb, to watch over me. I didn't choose to be born. I didn't choose to be white. I didn't choose my race, my forebears, my intellectual capacity, or my genes. These inherited blessings became mine at birth. It seems to me, Lord, you were often tugging at the strings of my heart, calling me to trust you even when I couldn't find the answer to complex questions and situations.

Out of a box of 50 used books, one just happened to be Letters from Aunt Charlotte—the same book my classroom teacher was reading to us. This book helped to introduce me to the Christian faith.

When I was totally convinced that I had no talents to share with others, you immediately proved me wrong by showing me I was gifted in intercessory prayer.

You put it in the heart of the good people of Immanuel Baptist Church of Savannah to send me to Ridgecrest Baptist Assembly where Spirit-filled speakers enlarged my understanding of what it means to follow you.

When my dream of being able financially to go to college seemed out of reach, you brought Leona Althoff into my life with just the message I needed to hear.

You never gave up on me! You encouraged my faltering good efforts and lavished me with forgiveness for my many fallible ways.

Your holy laughter chides my sometimes sanctimonious, know-it-all attitudes and responses.

You put up with my string of questions, my endless doubts, and persistence in straying.

You wrap me in a cocoon of love and acceptance.

You help me to accept those things I can't factually explain. Accepting your impossible acts with awe brings joy to my heart, hope to my life, and a song to my lips.

> The wonder of the Incarnation can only be accepted with awe. Jesus was wholly human, and Jesus was wholly divine. This is something that has baffled philosophers and theologians for two thousand years. Like love, it can't be explained, it can only be rejoiced in.—Madeleine L'Engle

---

*In 2021, a few months before I had received my Covid-19 vaccines, I was watching a Zoom worship service from my church, First Baptist of Chattanooga, Tennessee. Reggie Alley and Jordyn Parker sang "There Was Jesus," the work of American Christian rock musician Zach Williams and American singer-songwriter Dolly Parton.*

*Hearing that song became an unexpected holy encounter for me. Through my tears I sobbed, "That's exactly how it has been with me. Even when I didn't know it, Jesus was and is always there with me." Following are some of the words of that song:*

*In the waiting, in the searching*
*In the healing and the hurting*
*Like a blessing buried in the broken pieces*
*Every minute, every moment*
*Where I've been and where I'm going*
*Even when I didn't know it or couldn't see it*
*There was Jesus*

*On the mountain, in the valleys*
*There was Jesus*
*In the shadows of the alleys*
*There was Jesus*
*..........*
*Always is and always was*
*No, I never walk alone*
*..........*
*There was Jesus*

CPSIA information can be obtained
at www.ICGtesting.com
Printed in the USA
BVHW030855180722
642395BV00017B/539